RASH DECISIONS

Make peace with your past.
Accept where you are, and then
...Be Amazing.

RASHMI BISWAS

BALBOA.
PRESS
A DIVISION OF HAY HOUSE

Balboa Press books may be ordered through booksellers or by contacting:

Balboa Press
A Division of Hay House
1663 Liberty Drive
Bloomington, IN 47403
www.balboapress.com
1-(877) 407-4847

ISBN: 978-1-4525-4508-0 (sc)
ISBN: 978-1-4525-4507-3 (e)

Library of Congress Control Number: 2011963546

Because of the dynamic nature of the Internet, any web addresses or
links contained in this book may have changed since publication and
may no longer be valid. The views expressed in this work are solely those
of the author and do not necessarily reflect the views of the publisher,
and the publisher hereby disclaims any responsibility for them.

The author of this book does not dispense medical advice or prescribe the use
of any technique as a form of treatment for physical, emotional, or medical
problems without the advice of a physician, either directly or indirectly. The
intent of the author is only to offer information of a general nature to help
you in your quest for emotional and spiritual well-being. In the event you use
any of the information in this book for yourself, which is your constitutional
right, the author and the publisher assume no responsibility for your actions.

Any people depicted in stock imagery provided by Thinkstock are models,
and such images are being used for illustrative purposes only.
Certain stock imagery © Thinkstock.

Printed in the United States of America

Balboa Press rev. date: 1/26/2011

For my parents, Ann & Prasanta

If you want to make the gods smile,
tell them Your plans

TABLE OF CONTENTS

INTRODUCTION

Initially I planned to call this book "My Rear in Your View" but feared I might be sending the wrong message. January 2011 and it is *that* time of the year "The Year in Review" or in my case, "Your Rear in My View". This title is wholly appropriate partly because I am prone to slight dyslexia, never officially diagnosed so perhaps I am simply a poor reader. Example: two days ago I misread a TV news ticker tape advising that the actor Robert DeNiro had suffered a head injury. Reread slowly and it turns out Bob is heading up the jury at Cannes this year, bit of a difference but there you are.

Looking back to this time last year my day timer entry from Friday January 8, 2010 reads:

9am Sally update

1pm Conference call

House insurance follow up

Set goals for next 3 months—book, travel, work, exercise, network

5:30pm Optician

7:00pm Drinks with Tom & Pat

"Your Rear in My View" beyond the mild dyslexia, suits this book on a number of other fronts.

Today an email arrives informing that a guy from California is now following me on Twitter. Apparently he has all the answers to resolving bad credit. Does he know something I don't? Am I committing financial crimes without realizing? Financial fraud and frippery, or perhaps I am the victim of identity theft? I have always believed myself to be a bit of a fraud and admit that this in itself is a fraudulent comment. A smattering of self-deprecation, and as you can tell I can self-deprecate with the best of them, is de rigueur when a certain amount of success has abounded and humbly one pretends one doesn't think one deserves it while all the time one is silently screaming inside that it is "About Bloody Time." In truth I am with John Lennon when he said half of him thought he was a loser and the other half thought he was God Almighty. I think we all do. I am however sufficiently evolved to admit that I have always rather pretended to be something I am not. Not quite sufficiently evolved not to pretend of course. You see I always wanted to be clever, and frankly I am no slouch but I am not exactly PhD material as the University of Toronto was kind enough to point out, more on that later. This isn't about academia however; this is about facing up to who I really am, fraud and all, and, well, being ok with it.

In 2000 I worked for Budget Car Rental as a Corporate Trainer. Great job, heaps of travel and although based in Toronto I was delighted to find myself in the most obscure parts of the USA for weeks at a time. St. Charles, Illinois, Lemoore, California, Redding, California, Wichita Falls, Texas. Not really such obscure places but it was all new to me, and having moved to Canada from the UK in December 1996 (I am the type of person who moves to Canada in the winter, in for a penny, in for a face of frostbite and all that) every city and town in North America held a complete fascination for me and I was fortunate enough to travel across the USA and get paid for it. Not terribly well paid mind you but from an exploring and adventure perspective it was a fair exchange.

One Sunday I visited the Ewing Ranch, and as someone who spent her teen years watching "*Dallas*" and remembers cramming into the shabby common room at my halls of residence as a first year undergraduate to watch Bobby emerge from the shower, that Sunday afternoon in Plano Texas was a spiritual experience. On another weekend I took the stunning drive up to Yosemite National

Park, in a Crown Victoria no less and feeling very overdressed I might add. Taking a Crown Vic into a national park is probably the driving equivalent of attending a school fete in an evening dress and tiara or wearing fur to a PETA rally but there we are. In my Budget travelling days I loved the excitement of being at San Francisco airport on a Sunday afternoon, picking up a car at LAX under a California sunset, or flying back from Denver on a Friday night, even if occasionally my bags did not always follow. It felt glamorous, I felt glamorous, living a different life from anyone else I knew and different from the one I had imagined. My last day on the job with Budget was early April 2001 in Wichita Falls Texas. During the long drive back to Dallas, where I would catch my flight home, being careful to avoid the dead armadillos literally scattered, legs in the air, all over the road, and listening to David Gray inviting me to "Sail Away," I hear the voices of my now former colleagues override David's sweet tones with, "Happiness is Wichita Falls in Your Rear View Mirror." I think perhaps the locals had taken some creative license here as I have never been able to find the lyrics to such a song although they swore up and down it was a bone fide country song, "Yes Ma'am," however I suspect it is an adaptation, matters not. The point is I was looking back with glee, at Wichita Falls in my rear view mirror, brimming with excitement to be moving on, leaving it all behind and feeling confident that everything good lay ahead.

CHAPTER 1

You Cannot Get There From Here

"If we are facing the right direction, all we have to do is keep on walking."

Buddhist Proverb

January 15, 2010, today is my last day of employment with the company I have worked for since April 2003. I held two different roles in those seven years, each quite different from the other. The first as a learning and development manager, Head of Learning I liked to call it although that wasn't strictly accurate, and the second as a Regional Sales Manager for the Travel division. The latter position put me on a cruise ship for the first week of the job only for me to get off four days later in St Kitts to fly home to the UK for My Sister's 40th birthday do, as you do, well, as I do. Looking back I wonder if at that point they decided I wasn't sufficiently committed. I was, however, deeply committed and worked like a busy bee for five years, driving thousands of kilometers a month. I virtually lived in my car for half a decade, and in some really bad hotels in lovely-in-the-summer far reaches of Ontario. All along I was holding on for a promotion that frankly was never going to come, although I kidded myself it would for oh I don't know approximately 4 years, 5 months and 3 weeks. Good learning, some great people, a day in

Grand Cayman swimming with the stingrays and calling it work, all lovely however until I faced up to the harsh reality that my career was going nowhere. Flatlined, run out of gas, hit a wall, grounded, stalled, stuck, no liftoff, pick a cliché, it was dead in the water. To remedy this predicament I declared six months earlier that I would take up a longed-for PhD and study Human Resource Management until the proverbial cows came home, or until I was 50, whichever came first. In fact my Mother did comment that "Oh my god you'll be nearly fifty by the time you finish." My response at the time was "Well I will be fifty with or without a PhD." Thought I was very clever I did . . . .

I spent vast amounts of my free time in 2009 filling in forms, going to interviews, writing essays, obtaining references, digging out transcripts from years so long gone that the twelve year old administrator in the Manchester Metropolitan University records department exclaimed the files simply did not go back that far, "sorry." All very discomforting as I realized said administrator was not even a twinkle in her father's eye when I finished my second-class degree (2:2 to be in honest) in Hotel Management (don't ask) at what was then Manchester Polytechnic. Sheffield Hallam University having enjoyed my participation from 1992-94 were a little easier to deal with and it only took them four months, four international phone calls and numerous emails to provide the correct data which they then did so most obligingly, in octricate, if that is the correct term for providing 8 copies of something. As it turns out I rather wish they hadn't been quite so helpful in unearthing my grades as the Canadian university to which I was applying for my pursuit of higher learning decided my past achievements, including a Master's degree topped off with a rather insightful thesis into the gendered division of labour in the hotel industry with the brilliantly sexy title "Real Men Don't Make Beds," were not of sufficient academic standing, and my application to the PhD program either full or part-time was denied. Come on people, that is a great title, did you read the title?

I received this information from the University of Toronto in April 2010 having just returned from a rather splendid two week vacation with Lovely Husband to Costa Rica. There was *The Letter* among the huge pile of mail we had amassed since our departure. Sidebar, why do people only write to you when you are on holiday? I swear I barely receive a flyer from Good Luck Fitness when I am at home but the minute my back is turned the Posties descend. So, with the Restoration Hardware catalogues (we receive those in triplicate by the way) weighing down the kitchen table along with bills, bank statements, and bad marketing ideas, there was the miserable looking letter from U of T, immediately revealing its sad news contents by its skeletal appearance. Denied. My immediate reaction was fear, crikey, (yes I am in fact one of those people who still say crikey) what now? I quit my job because I told everyone I was going off to do a PhD. Might have been a tad premature looking back. Oh the shame, closely followed by its brother embarrassment and then swiftly followed by second cousin twice removed relief. Strange feeling that, to be relieved that something you thought you wanted and worked hard to achieve does not work out and good grief you are relieved? Crikey. This is where the behaviourists would encourage you to explore that feeling. So being something of a behaviourist myself, I did.

I was not however entirely without a Plan, dashed PhD hopes be damned. Lovely Husband had some eight months earlier embarked upon a new career as a self-employed Management Consultant and was doing rather well. We had agreed that when I left my job I would join him, at least for a few months, and together we would build the business beyond that of a one-man show. Immediately Lovely

Husband required my help with the design and delivery of some workplace training for one of his clients. After that first gig which took place one wintry weekend, and having received a few calls from folks in my network who were willing to hire me as an independent, I delighted in the idea of working with Lovely Husband and put my energies into growing Lake and Associates. I think subconsciously the pursuit of a PhD was simply a catalyst to force me to move on, prosper and change, and for that I am hugely grateful. And to paraphrase the poetic words of the Rolling Stones, while you may not get what you want, every now and again . . .

Within Lake one of our core beliefs, and incidentally the foundation of our early offering as a firm, is that businesses need to create and implement Plans. In fact we cite six reasons why leaders need to develop, and implement, a Plan:

1. A Plan Defines Direction
2. A Plan Puts You in Charge
3. A Plan Generates the Right Activity
4. A Plan Provides Momentum
5. A Plan Prioritizes Resource Allocation
6. A Plan Reduces Risk

1. A Plan Defines Direction

The classic illustration here, developed by Lovely Husband, is that we are all heading to Florida for the winter, an analogy that works well in this part of the world in February. If it is supposed to take us four days to arrive in Miami and at the end of day two we are only in Buffalo NY then clearly we have a problem. The reality is, just as I said to my Mother that I will be fifty with or without the PhD, we will all be somewhere at the end of the year but is it where you want to be? Thinking about and talking about your goals and ambitions is a great place to start. Saying out loud I am going to learn a language or run a marathon makes it all the more real. It does however start with knowing what you want. Do you know what you want? If not, try testing out a few ideas and by a process of elimination determine at the very least what it is that you don't want. It certainly worked for me. I knew I had to leave my job. I knew I did not want to trade one corporate badge for another; it was not for me at this stage, perhaps later on, who knows, but not now. I thought I wanted the PhD but in truth I was relieved when my application was rejected. All that being said, having a Plan helped enormously and I moved forward. And I learned the patience to appreciate that you may not go from A-Z in a perfectly straight line. I am taking a wiggly road, which is tough for a "J" (see Myers Briggs Type Indicator©) but it is working for me, when I let it.

Defining direction has been a staple in our house for the last six years, so it is no wonder we have built a business out of it. At the beginning of January Lovely Husband and I sit across from each other and write our personal goals for the year ahead:

From the Lake Blog November 22, 2010: What's In Your Freezer?

> *Later this week I will be showcasing our company at a breakfast meeting for the Niagara Area Business Women's Network (NABWN). As a member we each have the opportunity to participate periodically in a mini trade show prior to the meetings and of course most companies provide promotional materials, brochures and give-aways at that time. My give-aways for this week consist of freezer bags and a stack of post-it notes. Although definitely not glamorous, flashy or high tech this*

is a freebie worth having, providing you follow the instructions. For several years now in our house each New Year we take a set of coloured post-it notes and individually write our goals for the year, personal and sometimes professional. At some point on January 1 or 2 we read our individual post-its aloud to each other, compare notes, stuff each goal into a freezer bag and stash the lot on a shelf in the freezer. Why the freezer? Well, because we are in there at least every other day so we keep an eye on those purple, pink or green notes lying among the ice cream and the frozen peas, and these regular viewings help to keep the goals top of mind. Once in a while when we are cooking we will haul out the bag, re-read the notes and determine how far we are down the path in terms of achieving our goals, as we wait for the rice to boil. So far this approach has kept us on track with travel, renovations, exercise, cultural events and yes even cooking properly. While we do not recommend this approach for Business Planning, we do recommend it as a good start in helping create a discipline around identifying goals, writing them down, sharing them with others, and monitoring the progress.

2. A Plan Puts You in Charge

We advise our Clients that without a Plan, your customers, the competition, and coping with daily crisis, will all steer your business. Someone else will lead your business if you do not. Putting yourself in charge of your life is liberating, terrifying and frankly essential. For years I had allowed myself to be susceptible to the whims and expectations of others. As Lovely Husband notes, opinions are like ears, everyone's got them. Arguably a willingness to listen to others and be open to different perspectives is a sign of maturity.

The problem is that I listened to too many others, too closely, and failed to listen to myself. When I did listen to me it was simply to accommodate that negative Nellie constantly nagging at me that I was failing, underachieving, making the wrong choices and should in all likelihood have stayed in Britain, never left my family, and married that nice-boy-from-university who now runs a successful law firm, built a wine cellar that was featured in *Hello* magazine, and lives in the Cotswolds with a pack of golden retrievers.

Actually I received an out-of-the-blue voicemail from said Former Boyfriend a couple of years ago advising he would be in Toronto on vacation and wondered if I would like to meet for a drink. We had not laid eyes on each other or indeed had any contact whatsoever for almost twenty years. When I played the voicemail I felt like *"Martha"* picking up the phone only to hear Tom Waits at the other end of the line. I have not always made sensible decisions in my life however this time I did. I knew that however innocent the invitation and positive the intention no good could come of it and I deleted the message without replying. I love my Lovely Husband. Occasionally while driving up and down the QEW a few hundred times a month I have replayed the fictitious scenario of what would have happened if we had met for that drink. I often think this concept would make a fabulous short play and is oh so relevant given the growing number of fortysomethings tracking down exes on Facebook and the like. I have a couple of approaches to the reunion-evening-that-never-happened mainly revolving around what I am wearing, thank you Meg Ryan (*When Harry Met Sally*), and always looking completely fabulous, of course. The ending, however, is always the same. In my imagined scenario, during the course of the evening Former Boyfriend painfully laments our lifetime apart and literally begs me to run away with him back to Gloucester. I of course am completely unmoved by this outpouring of regret and emotion, nod kindly at his hopeful face across the candlelit table, gently and knowingly launching the line of all lines that if we had stayed together, his life would be just as it is now, exactly the same in fact, just with me in it. Then I remind him, and myself, that we broke up when we were 22 and I left him for a French waiter whose name I forget.

My friend Luke says, with a hollow laugh, that as he checks his lottery ticket on a Sunday morning an unwelcome but persistent voice in his head whispers "*Loser*" in a vile growl as the numbers displayed are not reflective of the numbers he was looking for. There, how is that for your self-esteem? I am sadly familiar with that voice, lottery tickets notwithstanding. I have worried and second-guessed. I have envied and reviled. I have retreated and withdrawn. But worse of all I have wasted time listening to those people (with ears) who in all fairness were making a throw away comment that I, bloody idiot, took to heart and carried with me or acted upon while those with ears were long gone and getting on with their lives. Me, I was stuck. To be able to forge ahead and get on in the face of immense criticism is what sets apart the winners from the non-winners. See Lady Gaga and Madonna for details. I admire those women in particular who ignore the Nelly in their head, and the Nellies around them, and do it anyway. What was that book we all read in university? *Feel the Fear and Do It Anyway.* If only I had read it to the end. To put myself in charge I needed a Plan.

3. A Plan Generates the Right Activity

It is completely amazing to me how busy we have become, or perhaps more accurately how busy we say we have become. I am sure we could all shave hours off our day if we stopped tweeting, checking our email every 3 minutes and generally working on the wrong stuff. Sure, everyone is busy, but busy doing what? I swear Obama has more free time than some of the people I know. But the key question is whether all this activity is helping us to get ahead. Doubtful. We are poorer than our parents, our kids spend more time in day care than our Fathers did at the office and our debts are rising. We are fatter, angrier, losing our memories in midlife and generally scoring a C- on the health, fitness and happiness scale. We are, as popular culture proclaims, the *Distracted Society*. Without trying to depress everyone beyond belief there is hope. Old adages are old for a reason, largely because they make sense and have stood the test of time. So here is the oldest of adages (sadly I have no idea who to attribute it to) "Plan your work and work your plan." With full respect to a dive teacher I had in 1999 who advised the class to always "Plan the dive and dive the plan." Wise words. Not a difficult concept really and I suspect I could have taken 250 pages to share that with you but here it is in Chapter One. We the *Distracted Society* are of course too busy to Plan . . . but we do have time to *Keep Up With the Kardashians* vote for *Idol* contestants and comment liberally on Hollywood cellulite, divorces and deaths, and other such important news fodder. So if you don't feel you have the time to make a Plan, switch off your TV, your phone and your laptop, sit down, and make a start. Then share it, stick to it and revisit it. Done. Like. Dinner. Should you be unfortunate enough to suffer a head injury on the way into work one Monday morning, the Plan will tell everyone in your organization, including you, exactly what should be done today. Aren't we looking for easy ideas and foolproof solutions? Well that my friends is one right there. As the running shoe people say, "move your arse."

4. A Plan Provides Momentum

What motivates you? A time honoured question posed to business leaders, non-profit advocates, mountain climbers, long distance runners, and long suffering second chairs in all walks of life. Responses can be thoughtful, trite, witty or all of the above. In practice, when we are knocked off course, veering into a slowdown, lockdown, and even showdown, what motivates us is sometimes a mystery even to ourselves. Yes, we all know climbers claim to climb mountains because "they are there" but at 1400 ft in the freeze-your-nose-off weather drenched in Lake District rain with soggy socks and slippery hair what on earth keeps a person going? I would suggest it is the Plan that keeps them going. I said I was going to do this so I bloody well will, I-have-started-so-I'll-finish sort of attitude. A fear of failure, or the desire to succeed, it doesn't really matter which it is as long as the motivation was there in the first place. So here's a thought; if you cannot find the time and or the motivation to write the Plan, how / where will you find the strength to keep going when the tent blows away and the tin opener drops silently into the dark gully below? Ironic isn't it that the Plan is what will push us to the end and provide the momentum as we struggle on. On the brighter side, the Plan also provides momentum because you celebrate the milestones as you work your Plan. A little positive reinforcement via small wins goes a long way with not only your staff but with you too.

From the Lake Blog September 27, 2010: Let's Start with Breakfast

> *"Let's start with breakfast" were the wise words spoken by Tessa Wilson, a fitness expert who participated in one of our Planning workshops last week. Essentially Tessa was suggesting that the good intentions we all have to improve our health, for example getting up at 4am and running 5km everyday, are more likely to be successful if we start small and focus on something we can*

achieve. This also absolutely applies to Business Planning. Not to say we should shy away from aiming high, however when we start with manageable actions, that we know we can commit to, we will be rewarded in the short-term and also lay the foundations for the longer-term success.

5. A Plan Prioritizes Resource Allocation

There is never enough money for all the projects and there is never enough time, see number 3. Aside from its application to business planning, resource allocation is a critical life skill. Go ahead and Google time management and then tell me that we don't have trouble prioritizing our resources. Often we are talking about financial allocations when it comes to resource prioritization and this is of course the underlying message in point number 5 from a business perspective. By having a Plan one can assign resources to projects with greater clarity and ease as the strategy has been set and the priorities have been identified, and, equally importantly, agreed to. Of course this is rarely as straightforward as it sounds here but by establishing clear criteria the element of guesswork is removed along with the emotional side of the decision making process. Similarly in our private lives allocating finances can be a cause for consternation. At a party we attended over the Labour Day weekend a few months ago discussion turned to the realities of back-to-school and one guest announced that with his daughter now heading off to university he would not be taking a vacation or changing his car for the next 4 years. This is a realistic and familiar challenge for many.

Everyday Life Decisions = Prioritization Problem
Finite Resources

11

Beyond the bank account however, what about "You" as a resource, made up of various currency components, stocks and investments? How do you prioritize the resources that are entirely precious, completely unique and readily available at your immediate disposal, i.e. You? The "You Resource" might be underappreciated, suffering from neglect, frequently overlooked, and rarely prioritized. On the other hand your "You Resource" maybe fully invested, cleverly allocated and delivering spectacular returns with interest. Either way what does "You" as a resource look like? No question you have skills, knowledge, intellect, compassion, empathy, fearlessness, creativity, drive, ambition, and on and on ad infinitum. Have you stopped to take stock of your "You Resources" lately? Much more than your resume, this is digging deep into who you are and where your passions, dreams and motivations lie. With a nod to Myers-Briggs Type Indicator © and spoken like a true "J" simply start with a list. Identify your "You Resources" and figure out what is available. This can be a bit like rooting around in the back of your wardrobe only to find that great jacket you could have sworn you had mistakenly sent to Goodwill last spring. We have so many talents, connections, and hidden depths available to us and yet we rarely try them on for size. As we move through our days on autopilot we ignore the untapped potential and even forget we possess such potential. If you have ever heard someone, or yourself, comment that "I used to be a really good singer/dancer/squash player and I don't really remember why I gave it up" then you know exactly what I mean.

Once you have listed the "You Resources" prioritize them based upon the goals you want to achieve, the Plan you have in your vision, the needs, the situation, and the energy you have for making all of this work. Ask yourself what the circumstances demand, and equally importantly what you feel like giving, and then go for it. Put your energy into your top "You Resources" to accomplish a goal that matters to you and watch yourself take flight in the process. Whether you get there today, tomorrow or next year is another matter entirely, however the simple process of road testing lost or forgotten expertise and muscles is a journey worth taking.

In January 2010 I discovered the latent "Me Resource" of self-discipline. It sort of crept up on me, which sounds a bit incongruous for a discipline resource I admit, but truly this is the way it happened. I was spending less time running around the province of Ontario now that I no longer left the house each morning to go out to work as a Regional Sales Manager, and in spite of having practically lived in my car for five years, suddenly the impact to my physical self was much worse than driving all day. I was literally sitting, all day, in front of a laptop inside my own house. No longer even walking the ten steps to the car. No longer walking down the mall to the food court, however, granted there are some nutritional advantages to having your own kitchen on hand during the day for real food. And if you are anything like me, working from home means you are never very far from a fridge literally and mentally. My Plan now included careful food monitoring, perhaps a little obsessively, and with equal vigour and commitment I rediscovered the joy of yoga. Without overstating it, yoga has changed my life. In 2010 I went to 159 yoga classes, spending approximately 200 hours on my purple mat, one tenth of a normal working year spent in downward dog and the like. This may not impress those who run 5 miles a day, everyday, however for me coming from a point of not having exercised for almost six years, save the odd walk with my dog, it was indeed significant. Exercise became a new commitment. I had been a corporate cog, focused on the job, the long hours, oh and did I mention the driving? And oh yes did I mention the commute? At one point in my previous life we moved from downtown Toronto, where we lived a mere 6km from the office, to Niagara which was a whopping 120km on the other side of the lake. Yes we were indeed quite mad and I soon began to watch *Location Location Location* rigid with fear, willing the participants to think very carefully before making the move from Islington to that picturesque Welsh mountain village. "Visit for god's sake" I screamed at the telly. "Don't move! Just enjoy sexy weekends away in quaint country hotels." "Why would you want to leave the City for good?" It has worked out well for us now five years on, but there were times when I questioned the sanity of that decision. Actually I still have a mini meltdown about every six months declaring that I cannot live without the City and to be truthful if Lovely Husband were willing to move back to said City I would have a board on the lawn faster than Phil Spencer could speed dial the agent.

Following our move to the "other side of the lake" I became well acquainted with dawn, short nights, and on the bright side, no line-ups at the Tim Horton's drive thru. If I was heading to a meeting in Toronto my day now involved getting up at 4:30am arriving at the office by 7am and returning home around 7pm. I rarely endured this more than once a week mind you as I worked in the region, although Lovely Husband silently suffered through it daily for a couple of years. Eat. Sleep. Repeat. And yes I do know lots of people who for a whole host of reasons stoically make such a trek everyday for years. Simply stated they are infinitely better men, women and "extreme commuters" than me, hats off.

For years and years I was miserable in my work. Okay not exactly *miserable* but not what you would call happy either. I would be the person who complained about her job to her friends at the weekend. My patient friends put up with me thankfully, but frankly I am not sure how or why. Looking back I was never super happy with any of the jobs I have had, and I have had several. The constant job hopping is arguably typical for a Gen Xer, I was born in 1967, or possibly indicative of continually seeking the next big opportunity, like a tenacious hog aching for the prize of truffles, or perhaps I was hell bent and determined that the perfect job was just around the corner, if only I looked a bit harder. I was a serial new hire. By stark contrast, Lovely Husband worked for the same company for 39 years. Will that ever happen again? I wonder if the Millenials will follow suit with life-long employment and close the circle? By the way what happened to Gen Y? Did they just morph into becoming the Millenials? Lucky ducks. Years ago when we were anxiously studying and reporting on the *"Demographic Time Bomb"* as it was euphemistically referred to in the journals, we were fully aware that Generation X were destined to be a blink, or is that a blip, on the landscape. We never really stood a chance, we didn't even warrant a proper name. Gen Xers became the last in the litter of cute labs that everyone just referred to absentmindedly as "Puppy" because all the good names were taken. Talking about the *"Demographic Time Bomb"* with such fear and gloom in 1990 seems as absurd as Y2K panic from the vantage point of 11 years on. But we did, didn't we? Although, in spite of discussing the perils of an ageing population widely for over two decades at least, I am not sure we have stockpiled the metaphorical torches, spare batteries and bottles of water in preparation.

I suspect, having given this hours of consideration, that what I was looking for with my furious career-changing habit was total life fulfillment, from a job. Tall order. And then in 2010 having released my death grip on becoming a corporate superstar I fell in love with yoga. I had flirted with yoga for a few years in the early 2000s and many people who knew me then would say I was addicted and I may well have been, frequently taking four yoga classes each weekend and all, but that was a different time and this time it was different. Yoga has literally changed my life by becoming an important part of my life, operative word being part. Yoga beyond the exercise (I have never had arms like this in my life by the way) is a passion, a lifestyle, and most importantly a way of viewing the world and oneself. Just take stock of your breathing for a moment. Close your eyes, sit up straight, and take a deep inhale through your nose and exhale every last breath before taking another inhale. When was the last time you managed to take a breath like that? Notice what you feel. Notice how your shoulders drop, how your mind clears and how a gentle smile appears on your lips. This is a joyous gift. I did 200 hours of that in 2010. Bliss. How can that not change you? I cannot pretend to the uninitiated that yoga is as easy as sitting upright in a chair, looking fabulous in the latest *Lulus* and breathing in and out through your nose with a beatific smile on your face. One doesn't achieve the prize of defined arms without work, as one might imagine, sorry. Jane and Bridget, to name two of the incredible teachers I practiced with, pushed me to limits I seriously doubted I could reach. And as Jane taught me to apply in practice, and in life, we must learn to "doubt our doubts." I would laugh in the early stages of my new found yoga exercise at the prospect of holding a one arm side plank with scissor legs for more than 3 seconds, or even at all. Or of sliding in an optional push-up in between vinyasas (not really optional at all however the illusion remains a comfort). Yet with good training, clear direction, and the emergence of my latent self-discipline I now consider these to be part of my regular practice. I can do it, and the Janes, Bridgets, Lucys and Ellens helped me, I wonder if they know?

From the Lake Blog December 17, 2010: Tell Me Something Good

With full respect to Rufus and Chaka Khan, "Tell Me Something Good." Today I ran into a woman who has made a big impact on me this year. We will call her Ms Impact. Up until today, Ms Impact had no clue that she had helped me immeasurably or that I admire and respect her talent, her approach to applying her skills, and her encouragement. She is a lovely person, an excellent teacher and likely the best coach I have been fortunate enough to encounter in 2010. Ms Impact has pushed me to do things I did not know I could do, in fact even thought I couldn't, and for that I am truly thankful. So today, when by chance, I met Ms Impact out and about doing her Christmas shopping, I told her. And it felt great. Take the opportunity in the Season of Goodwill to tell someone something good, what a gift, for you, and likely for them too.

Allow me to clarify; this is not a case of who can bench press more poundage than whom, this is about finding depths within, using determination, hard work and delighting in the pursuit for its own sake. This is about walking up the driveway after a Sunday morning hot yoga class and Lovely Husband telling me he can tell I have just returned from yoga as my face takes on a serenity that only comes with yoga practice, sweat and red cheeks aside. It is about calming down, taking time, focusing on what matters and My Sister telling me later in the year that I am a different person. My Sister thought it was due to leaving the endless pursuit for corporate career approval and the exhausting chase I was on to slay a corner office come hell or high heels. She could be right. I now know that I became a different person because I found and prioritized my "Me Resources" which may in fact amount to the same thing. I do know that My Sister is right, I am a different person, and I'm glad about that.

6. A Plan Reduces Risk

When working with clients we talk about risk reduction in terms of increasing certainty by following a Plan. Of not making the same mistakes again, and as far as possible eliminating uncertainty while living in the rapidly shifting world. Allow me to take you back to the scuba diving classes where we were taught that "planning your dive and diving your plan" can save your life. Risk reduction through planning in action, at 60 feet below the surface. I once had a wild-eyed underwater argument about changing a dive plan at 35 feet, and I would not recommend it. I left the corporate environment and a steady pay cheque, just as the rest of the world was bailing out Greece, foreclosing in Florida and generally tightening its global belt. There is never a good time to make life changes that might hurt, and there are always risks involved, however there are worse times. Oddly enough this was not the worst time. I had a Plan. Granted it did not work out exactly as I had imagined.

From the Lake Blog March 20, 2011: Business in Bloom by Planning Ahead

> *Yesterday, at the Canada Blooms exhibition in Toronto I listened to a presentation on How to take a Great Garden Picture. As I am dreaming of spring this was a lovely way to spend an hour or so on a sunny Saturday in March. The presenters, a professional photographer named Donna Griffiths, and Erin McLaughlin the editor-in-chief of Canadian Gardening magazine gave tips and advice on making the most of the natural light, encouraged us to not be afraid of lying on the ground to capture the best shot, and shared ideas on how to shoot verticals, vignettes, and macros. Although the technical expertise was helpful and the*

photographs stunning, the take-away for me (along with the reminder to keep the camera in the kitchen at the ready for those perfect early morning pics) was the importance of planning ahead. At Canadian Gardening magazine, we learned that all the photos are taken in the prior year. Of course, it makes perfect sense because if you want to feature April flowers and gardens on the front cover of the April 2011 magazine you are not going to be able to take those photos just in time for going to print. The entire magazine is literally shot the year before. Now that is planning.

CHAPTER 2
WHO ARE YOU?

"If I am not for myself, who will be?
And if I am for myself alone, then what am I?
And if not now, when?"

Rabbi Hillel, Pirkei Avot

Monday February 8, 2010 at 9pm the CBC National reports that
Colonel Russell Williams is taken in for questioning in connection
with assaults on women in the Trenton area. The TV shows a
handsome, smiling, capable looking man in razor sharp military
uniform. None of us can quite comprehend what we are seeing.
Tuesday February 9, 2010 at 9am I am sworn in as a Canadian
citizen and among the visiting dignitaries is a Canadian Forces
Airman. You could hear the sharp intake of breath from the audience
packed into the school auditorium as he stepped out on to the stage.
Brave man, it takes courage to wear that uniform on any given day
but on that morning, well, we can only imagine and we salute you.

From the Lake Blog May 10, 2010: Canadian Context

> *I am Canadian . . . a few weeks ago I became a Canadian*
> *Citizen. Having lived here for over 13 years no one could*
> *accuse me of rushing into this decision. The ceremony was*
> *well orchestrated, and welcoming. I did feel immensely proud,*

grateful, a little teary, and part of a bigger something. I like a sense of occasion and ceremony now and again, must be something to do with my British heritage. The presiding officials talked about diversity, leadership and everyone's role to play in making Canada a positive place to live. That we all have our role to play is absolutely true and how gratifying to really feel you are part of a bigger something and working for a greater good. Isn't that how leadership, management and coaching should make someone feel, every day? Ah if only we could. Ah, if only we would. As a practicing manager, what could we do every day to make someone feel significant, letting them know how much they are valued and that they matter, and their contribution matters? Our firm belief in terms of the answer to this goal is rooted in the importance of providing context. Setting context creates the bigger picture. Setting context shows a person the importance of what they are doing. Setting context provides meaning. Leaders provide context to show connections, identify dependencies, and to reveal the whole story. Without context there is no reason.

Becoming a Canadian citizen was an important moment for me. As a British Subject I am able to officially retain my Britishness and a European Union friendly passport. Dual citizenship is a curious privilege. When my Mother-in-Law, Charlotte, now Canadian, previously German, arrived in Canada in 1949 her citizenship was in question and she was summarily pronounced to be Stateless. I cannot imagine what this felt like for her or what leaving Europe for Canada in 1949 must have felt like for a Dutch man and a German woman with a small son in tow. Dual or rather duel citizenship?

For me, having two citizenships now seems rather greedy. My own Father left India for England in 1956. He arrived in London, fully qualified as a doctor, leaving behind his parents, two siblings, and numerous other rellies to study for his Fellowship. Suffice to say Father met Mother over an operating table, they married in 1962, had two daughters two years apart and he never returned to live in India. Regarding his own citizenship Father had to choose, and so relinquished his Indianess in order to become British. I think today he could have both. Today he could be greedy like me.

My Sister and I were fortunate to visit our Grandparents' home in India (complete with curious purple light bulb in the bedroom we shared) every few years. Consequently my first flight was to New Delhi at the tender age of five in December 1972. One's first flight is a milestone at any age although no one could have had a more memorable maiden voyage than my Mother. For in December 1972, at the age of 35, she too was taking her first journey outside the UK. I think about that sometimes when I am packing to go on holiday even now. I wonder what that must have been like for her. Two small children, Christmas to pull together and pull off, pretending to be Santa leaving a sack full of presents, cooking a turkey, baking batches of mince pies, and then oh yes let's go to India for a month, and by the way you were born and raised in Lancashire and have never left Britannia's shores. Brave woman. I think she got sick. I really should ask my Mother for her recollection of that family vacation. I suspect it was not much of a vacation for her. All I remember is the peculiar lilac hue in the bedroom, exotic and mysterious mosquito nets, the smell of wood smoke, my delightful doting grandparents, and a rather fabulous pair of fur lined boots I wore for the outbound journey that were naturally redundant upon arrival. Heather Mallick observes in her charming book *Pearls in Vinegar* that a woman always remembers what she was wearing during the significant moments of her life.

One of the many things I like about living in Canada is that when someone asks me where I am from, and I say I am from England, they say "Ah lovely" or "Great" or "Cool" and more often that not "Oh yeah my grandfather came from Scotland." When I lived in England and someone asked me where I was from and I said I was from Blackpool, people would say "Yes but where are you really from?" I cannot say I remember encountering significant racism growing up in Blackpool in the 70s and 80s. Family friends called my Father "Biz" (short for Biswas) rather than use his given name Prasanta, which is not really a difficult name to pronounce. It is only with hindsight that I realize "Biz" in all likelihood was, and remains, a term of endearment, never intended to cause offence, nor was delivered with malicious intent. The children of family friends even went as far as to call him "Uncle Biz" and some still do even though they are now well into middle age themselves. I however, angry, poetry writing teenager that I was, allowed myself to be suitably outraged by this abbreviated nickname from time to time.

Thankfully I can count my overt encounters with racism on one hand. I do recall some playground nonsense as a small child attending Carr Head School in Poulton, and we all know kids are cruel. Beyond the basic stuff two clear incidents stand out as pointers to remind me that I was different, felt different and looked different. The first was when I was about eight years old. We were changing after P.E., and I was strangling myself with the maroon school tie and less than crisp white shirt collar trying to wriggle back into my uniform quickly before the next class and evidently failing miserably. With my collar sticking up and the tie in the process of being knotted, a teacher spotted me and advised that although he did not know which land I was from, here, this is how one dresses, and proceeded to correct my clothing errors. He may have been teasing, but as my cheeks flushed and embarrassment took hold, the message I received was clear enough.

The second memorable incident was a few years later when at the age of about sixteen I had stayed overnight on a Saturday with my school friend Janet Stevens who lived in Fleetwood, about five miles from where we lived in Poulton-le-Fylde. After breakfast on Sunday the Stevens family, plus me, went to their local church for morning service. As we entered the church Mrs. Stevens introduced me to the Vicar who took one look at me and said "So you have come to visit us here in civilization have you?" Without pausing for breath or thought and with a thunderous look in her eyes Mrs. Stevens shot back with "Poulton is actually quite civilized Vicar." I still love her for that, so thank you Mrs. Stevens, as I likely never told you how much your instinctive and protective response meant to me at the time.

In February 2010 I secured my first contract. Yes, agreed, I had worked with Lovely Husband in January but that was his Client and I hadn't landed that gig by myself. In early February I went to my first Client meeting, submitted my first proposal (which incidentally took me an entire weekend to write) and on the appointed day arrived with flipcharts, *Mr. Sketch* smelly pens, post-it notes, and a full deck of slides to conduct my inaugural day as a self-employed Management Consultant. I had spent hours preparing. I was terrified. I was fabulous (even if I say so myself). Enormous relief. Most welcome positive feedback. Just as well. I had a lot riding on this. Here after all was the rubber hitting the road on my new adventure, and as a colleague commented recently, in this business "you eat what you kill."

Marcus London, the faith-in-me Client, asked me back for further work so I took this to be a good sign. I think Marcus (who knew me from a previous life) had more confidence in me than I had in me. It was the most amazing compliment. I remain grateful to Marcus for giving me my first opportunity as an independent practitioner. Nor shall I forget the moment later in the year, when, once again working with the same group, they warmly declared me to be one of the team. Was that a bad thing? Had I gone native? Matters not. All in all this was a fairly quick reinvention from Regional Sales Manager to independent Organizational Development Consultant. The best part being that I was starting to figure out that this is what I am good at and this is what I should be doing.

From the Lake Blog October 12, 2010: Never Going to Be a Ballerina

As a trainer at heart I remain acutely aware that despite the best learning program, or the most focused coaching, some people will outperform the others. Even with a level playing field some will be able to "Bend it like Beckham" while others are destined to warm the bench. The question is whether this is a sad reality or on the other hand, liberating. I choose to view this as a freeing reality. Little Rashmi, aged 5, eager and willing, yet rotund, clumsy and uncoordinated, and despite her Mother's encouragement, was never going to be a ballerina. This has become a reality check for me in adult life, which doesn't mean I don't try many different sports, experiences and activities (remind me to tell you about the time I tried to learn the Tabla) and I have even enjoyed several different careers. I have however come full circle back to my true calling as a trainer, facilitator, and presenter. Identifying, and then doing what you are good at is a search for all of us, but a search worth pursuing.

Meeting new people has never been something I relish or look forward to. I am of course fascinated to meet new people but I am an "I" after all (see Myers Briggs Type Indicator©) and unknown social settings can fill me with dread, fear and exhaustion. Often when I am facilitating a session, or running a training event, participants consider me to be a natural and easygoing extrovert. Not so. I can of course, as a fully-fledged grown-up woman, hold my own in a range of situations and you can in all likelihood take me anywhere. I am comfortable with the front-line and the boardroom. Just don't ask me to go to a party where I don't know anyone, or worse where I know a few people a bit. Above all do not, please, do not, throw me into a networking event. It is because of this somewhat (okay mildly raging) anti-social streak that I have in my past accepted social invitations only to cancel my appearance at the last minute. Shameful behaviour I admit, and now that I consider myself to be cured of this social disorder and all round bad form I deplore this conduct in others. As we say in our house now "if it's on the calendar, you're going."

I have been known to not answer the phone, even when I know who is calling. In fact I would rather not answer the phone at all if it could be avoided. Lovely Husband is usually Chief Phone Answerer in our house, if he happens to be out then voicemail is all you're getting. Email was made for me, unbearably shy loner that I am. Shy or rude? This can be a fine line. Aloof or coy? Unfriendly or cautious? Detached or demure? Best not to ponder for too long.

Venturing into unknown territory does not scare me in itself, after all I am the serial new hire who has lived in three countries (if you count Scotland, which most people do) and tried her hand at a myriad of sports, instruments, hobbies, languages and volunteer scenarios. No, it is the social setting bit that makes my blood run cold. Add to this the fact that I generally arrive early for each and every appointment, a firmly entrenched slightly Obsessive Compulsive trait that cannot be undone. Given my insistence upon premature arrival I bear the burden of a curious self-inflicted house-party-blend of misery of not wanting to be somewhere because I am going to have to talk to people I don't know coupled with arriving first so that I am absolutely the only available target for the next guest who pulls up at the bar. I suspect I need to learn to arrive much later, late in fact, and walk into a crowded room, which, I admit after years of social experimentation, is far easier than walking into an empty space and awaiting the inevitable. When in the midst of a crowd just carry something authoritatively across the room and you will look as if you fit right in. My Sister, who, enviably, is one of the most highly socially skilled people I know, advises that when she is at a party where she knows no one she ploughs in and offers to help, turning strangers into friends as she passes the canapés. Sidebar, I never tire of being school-girlishly amused at the idea of serving someone a can-of-peas for the appetizer, something to do with a Lancashire background and all that.

I mentioned earlier that I am cured of my crippling social ineptitude. I like to think this is the case and in 2010 made extensive efforts to walk head held high and doubting my doubts into networking events, meetings, conferences, Feldenkrais workshops, and all manner of training classes. I became a joiner. Wednesday February 24, 2010, 7:30am I attend a women's networking group meeting in my area called NABWN. Deep breath, knockout coat that cost me two weeks salary in 2002 and still looked fabulous (I should bloody well hope so), big smile, chin up (of course) and I walked into a room full of strangers.

Not only did I live, of course, but I actually enjoyed myself. I met wonderful women, interesting people who were in return interested. I sat at a table of eight for breakfast and spoke to everyone.

I exchanged business cards. "Eat what you kill" echoing in my mind. This had nothing to do with the breakfast I was about to consume, but rather one cannot survive as a self-employed person without networking. It is the lifeblood for an entrepreneur. It is our oxygen. Tim Sanders, whom I adore and perhaps have had a slight crush on since hearing him speak in Orlando in 2004, insists that as *Lovecats* our network is indeed our "net worth." Introverts take heed, the man Sanders is right. If you have not had the pleasure of reading *Love is the Killer App* by the fabulous Tim Sanders, then bluntly, you should.

I suspect, in fact I know, that I am not alone in my aversion to networking events. We enroll, sign our names, pay our fees, and all with good intentions. With every intention in fact of enlisting to the Executive Committee and gradually taking over the world. Over time however we create an inbox full of extremely good reasons why we cannot possibly attend. The excuses are not the I-am-short-of-time-can't-make-it-can't-believe-I-will-miss-it old chestnut, but rather the I-simply-would-rather-not-go-even-though-I-know-I-should garden-variety excuse that typically dare not speak its name. Our report card at this juncture pointedly comments that "little Joanie lacks discipline." No discipline. The social equivalent of not opting for the salad because the wings look so damned good. Of lying on the sofa claiming and feigning a slight sore throat rather than reaching for the stretch pants and rolling out your yoga mat. Are most of us just laggards at heart? Is it just me? God I hope it isn't just me. Or rather, it used to be me. Believe me I don't mean to sound smug but remember 2010 was the year I took control, felt the fear and did a headstand. Susan Jeffers would be proud of me.

Consequently I joined NABWN and as the great Blue Rodeo proclaim, "Never look(ed) back." I went to a NABWN plant exchange in June, which was a first for me and definitely not my usual social gathering. I spent large parts of that afternoon humming and ha-ing declarations of far too busy etc until Lovely Husband thrust a newly potted Hosta cutting into my hand and requested I bring back anything except another Hosta as we were overrun with their leafy offerings, unless it was a blue one as he loves the blue ones. Apparently I was going to the plant exchange.

From the Lake Blog June 27, 2010: Show Up

> *Woody Allen is quoted as saying that 80% of success is attributed to simply showing up. I participated in a networking event one evening last week and the next day received a phone call inviting me to give a presentation to the same group at their next meeting. I was likely going to be asked to present at some point given the nature of the group however I am convinced I was approached sooner rather than later because I was at the networking event the night before, because I showed up. Whether a business owner, a manager, or an entrepreneur, this applies, think what you can achieve by simply showing up. Sam Walton founder of Wal-Mart famously commented that if you want to know what is wrong with your business ask your front-line. Show up this week and see what it does for you.*

February was connection month. I made all manner of appointments to meet acquaintances, friends, former colleagues and new contacts for lunch, coffee, cups of tea, quick chats, and long catch-ups. I kept all of these appointments. Others did not. It was a revelation to me having left the corporate world, how the employed view the now self-employed. I received the oddest reactions from the most unlikely sources. CEOs I did not really know all that well sent me generous emails and good wishes out of the blue inviting me to seek their counsel and support whenever needed, they declared how excited they were for me and offered to help if they could, just call. I did, and you know what, they did too. Impressive. What surprised, shocked, and at times even hurt my fragile ego, were those folks with whom I had worked more closely, who continued to encourage me to schedule time with them and always cancelled at the last minute. Wait, that's my thing, or rather was my thing. We know as trainers, consultants, managers, and leaders, we are only ever as good as our last time up to bat. Other professions successfully manage to avoid this trap. If Colin Firth makes a lousy movie (perhaps a bad example as I don't know that CF has it in him to make a bad movie but hypothetically) all would be forgiven and on he goes due to the stellar body of work comprising his whole career. Seems fair enough to me not to be judged, tried and hanged for one minor offence. This luxury is not available to most. We are remembered, fondly or otherwise, for our last performance. Human Resource types refer to this as the "recency effect" particularly when it comes to annual reviews. Only the latest, greatest and truly awful stand out. And on these events, outbursts or accomplishments, we are assessed. Think about how easily, and tragically, reputations can be ruined. One badly timed tantrum, a lapse in self-control, a slip of the mask, can all land us in the "difficult section" or worse, "used to be really good just don't know what happened to her" column. Sad, but true. Beware cancellers for this is how you shall be remembered. I should know.

Networking events did not always pan out as planned. At one particularly memorable dinner event I ran into a group of acquaintances. Upon learning of my new chosen path, the jury was fairly evenly split between "wow, good for you, tell me all about it" and "oh, you're a vendor now, aaggh I hate receiving calls from vendors." Do people sometimes forget to filter? What ever happened to being Canadian and painfully polite at all costs? There are times when a person needs this stereotype fulfilled. Come on people, play the game. Do I look fat in these pants should not be answered with "well you don't look fat in *those* pants."

Talking of looking fat in those pants, if we are what we eat then it was time to find out exactly what I was made of. With this in mind I took the brave step and began recording my daily food and drink intake (now there is an eye opener). My Sister, who had a couple or three years earlier shaken a few pounds on Weight Watchers, and kept it off I might add, swears by the power of the pen against the battle of the bulge, all hail the food diary. Like many others, and women in particular, I have long suffered a love-hate relationship with food. I loved to eat and in turn hated the way I looked. I was a round child, slimmer teen, but UK size 14 nonetheless (big boned I think was the expression at the time) however at university I truly ballooned. A "Smiths" fan, along with half of my generation at the time, and firmly under the influence of Morrissey and "Meat is Murder" I became vegetarian at the age of 20 and remained a vegetarian for ten years. I am not blaming M for my weight gain, that was all my own work, more on the Vegetarian Years later, first the fat thing.

As a first year undergraduate I lived in halls of residence, and meals were provided. The meals were completely awful and I compensated in five-star student style. Late night kebabs, chocolate chip cookies (at my lowest ebb/ heaviest weight I purchased and consumed a full bag of cookies everyday on my way home from class) wholesale boxes of Kit-Kat, and naturally, the drink of choice for all undergraduates in the Greater Manchester Area in the late 80s, Boddingtons beer.

In my defense, (don't laugh) I did not possess a full-length mirror, but my ever shrinking jeans should have been a clue. I rather ignored the fact that I was morphing into an elephant, and kept on eating. Snickers bars at the bus stop first thing in the morning (or were they still Marathon bars in 1987?) immediately followed by a breakfast of sugary cereal and two slices of plastic white bread in the cafeteria; hot chocolate and scones for lunch; cheese and biscuits before supper (while involved in the process of cooking supper) and then supper itself consisting of pasta or rice of feed-a-family-of-four gigantic proportions. When I became veggie, if you can believe it, my diet actually deteriorated further. So even though I kicked the kebab habit, the mounds of carbs and chocolate could not keep up with my sedentary lifestyle. I had left school playing hockey, tennis, horse riding every Saturday, dabbling in a bit of netball (although always wing defence and actually not very good) but when I went off to university dragging all my sporting equipment with me in my 1976 bronze Honda Civic, I never actually darkened a pitch, court, pool or stables. I did play squash, twice, and joined an aerobics class at a Church Hall in Withington where I really got my money's worth and went three times.

I knew at the time I was fat, and I was also deeply miserable. But I didn't really know that bit. No surprise there. No one eats Thornton's chocolate truffles by the pound to stave off hunger, and if you can consume enough ice cream so that your tongue actually becomes numb there is a point of realization where you are scoffing down hundreds of calories by the mouthful and you cannot actually taste anything. So by this stage eating isn't even a guilty pleasure, it is just guilty as one does not inhale a litre of creamy vanilla without reflecting back on this appalling behaviour the next morning as you toss out the licked-clean carton accompanied by shed loads of eater's remorse.

I began to hate myself, which as you can appreciate was not the ideal response to the situation. Solution. Bulimia. Of course, this was the natural progression, why hadn't I thought of it earlier? As all the stats and research will tell you, women who diet are significantly more likely to become bulimic than women who do not diet. And I was a diet queen. Every week or so, finally disgusted with my bulk, I would venture to the supermarket, Gateways in Withington to be precise, make a pledge to a cottage cheese, with pineapple, and low fat yoghurt menu for the entire week. I would buy four tubs of cottage cheese, with pineapple, and a dozen pots of fat free black cherry yoghurt, only to gorge on almost all of it by the end of the day. Short-lived commitment. Needless to say, this somewhat unorthodox approach to weight loss proved to be unsuccessful. Square one, square arse, squashed confidence. Miserable. At one point I weighed in at a hefty 182 lbs, or 13 stone in Brit speak. Big boned indeed at 5' 7". Actually I don't know why I bother telling you my height, you would have to be a giraffe to carry off 13 stone or 182 lbs with panache. Now I weigh 136lbs, 132lbs if I have been ill, and up to 139lbs over the (or any excuse) festive season. Unsurprisingly I am still 5' 7". The key difference, apart from the mystery of the missing 46lbs, is that I am no longer miserable. I am happy. I enjoy my work, I practice yoga, I keep a food diary, and oh yes, I buy great clothes that I can just about afford so I have every incentive to keep on wearing them. And, I am in possession of a well-lit full-length mirror. I finally gave up on vegetarianism at the age of 30. To this day I remain slightly ashamed that I fell off the anti meat wagon after spending ten years tightly seat-belted into it. If I was to be even a remotely healthy eater as a vegetarian then I had to cook properly. The one bedroom 600 square foot apartment on Isabella Street, Toronto with a kitchen the size of a dog bed was no place to cook. We ate out. Bring on the meat. Which in turn contributed to bringing on the weight loss as I no longer rewarded myself with two bagels because I wasn't having the tuna or ham, which trust me was an argument I had with myself (and lost or won depending on how you look at it) on many occasions.

I have a lovely cousin Sasha, who lives in Paris. Sasha is not only without a shadow of a doubt the absolutely cleverest person I know but Sasha is also the only woman I know who at 50 plus can eat cake everyday (although not in a Marie Antoinette kind of way) and not wear it the next. Yet, when Sasha lived in England for a couple of years, to read English at Cambridge, she confided to me that she gained the most weight of her life. Sasha and I talked about this once and concluded, based on a sample of two women with similar genes, that living in England makes you fat. Lots of ex-pats now living in Canada claim they would *love* to move back to the UK but simply can't afford to, financially. Me, I can't afford the calories.

A Typical Sampling from the 2010 Food Diary

<u>Monday</u>

- All Bran, muesli, blueberries, milk
- Tin of tuna, 1 teaspoon mayo, carrots, cherry toms, raw cauliflower
- Chicken breast, curried with peas and spring onion
- 1 teaspoon peanut butter

<u>Thursday</u>

- 1 scrambled egg, 1 rasher bacon
- Tin tuna, 3 x baby beetroot, 1 teaspoon mayo, carrots, raw cauliflower
- Half tin of chickpeas
- 2 glasses of wine
- yoghurt and blueberries
- 2 teaspoons peanut butter

<u>Friday</u>

- Latte, oatmeal, blueberries, milk
- Arugula salad, toms, nuts, cheese
- Blueberry muffin
- 2 glasses of wine
- Chicken breast, mushrooms, cauliflower
- Half cup frozen yoghurt

An A-Typical Sampling Reads:

<u>Saturday</u>

- All Bran, muesli, blueberries, milk, many grapes
- 3 x ham slices, 2 x chicken tandoori slices, carrots, toms, celery
- 10, 000 peanuts, 3 glasses wine, lots of bubbles
- 1 x sausage, half tin of baked beans, 1 x chicken leg
- ½ cup frozen yoghurt
- 1 teaspoon Nutella
- Stop the nuts!!!!!

Fat Rashmi is never very far away. She lurks in the background waiting to reclaim my body and my wardrobe, tossing my self-esteem into the garbage as she does so. I know of course that she is I, and I am she. Friends who have had babies comment on how when they were pregnant complete strangers felt it was well within their rights to comment on the changing body shape of a woman with child. I have never been pregnant but I can identify with this as a former fat person. When I was big I received direct and indirect comments all the time from all kinds of people, some of who were supposed to love me.

Once, in a Manchester pub called the *Barleycorn*, a drunken tosser, who was chatting up my friend, turned to me and asked if I was a Maori, which is one of those comments that succeed in insulting and humiliating so many and at so many levels. That we are a thin obsessed society is of course the ultimate understatement, and worse we treat fat people as lesser beings. I am not preaching the virtues of slenderness. I believe in the freedom of choice and find all manner of body types attractive and appealing. What I do know is that I have been fat and I have been not fat. I know which one I prefer.

On a recent flight from Vancouver to Toronto I was seated in my pre-booked aisle seat with an exceedingly small woman next to the window and an empty seat in between us. Just when you think you are home free and will be able to stretch out an extra 2.5 inches, the third passenger hurries towards us, waving a boarding pass in our direction which indicates she is to occupy the middle seat. The woman is attractive, young, perhaps 25 years old, well dressed, and looks as if she easily weighs in at over 300lbs. The poor woman could barely squeeze her size into the middle seat and of course her body literally spilled over into the seats of window lady and me. This was to be an armrest up flight, which after almost forty years of flying was a first for me. I won't pretend that I didn't mind this physical intrusion into my territory and having to touch another person (without choosing to) for five hours made for an unpleasant journey to say the least. When we landed in Pearson after a supremely uncomfortable flight, I thought about Fat Rashmi, and how although I had been inconvenienced for a short time, I would disembark from this aircraft and walk away. This young woman in 29E was not so fortunate. She walks away carrying that enormous body with her. I no longer felt sorry for me.

This is in no way a diet book. However, as a woman who lost 46lbs and has essentially kept it off now for the best part of 14 years I have a couple of ideas to share on the subject:

1. Mentally imagine nutritious food as joy and all the rest as pain. Chips, cookies and processed foods are not going to help and they are going to hurt. Why do it to yourself?
2. Weigh yourself. None of this "oh I can tell by my clothes" nonsense. Pounds are pounds. Face the truth, make a Plan, and act upon it.
3. Invest in a full-length mirror, and look at yourself often from the front and the rear, naked, yes with your glasses on, and yes in harsh overhead lighting. Remember to close the blinds.
4. View your calorific intake positively. For example, "I have 1200 calories to enjoy today" rather than "uggh I'm on a diet and am only *allowed* 1200 calories."
5. Find out why and when you overeat by tapping into your feelings when you reach for the crap that isn't even real food. Write it down. A pattern will emerge. If you are miserable, start there, or maybe you are just bored.

6. If you fall off your healthy eating wagon let it go and catch the next one without blame, shame, or guilt.

7. Do you really want food or in fact do you need to drink something? Make a cup of tea first and find out before you reach for a slice of cake. I have discovered a world of delicious teas and am currently the number one fan of Presidents Choice Choccie and Mint, which is splendid. If I live near you, I am afraid your branch of Loblaws maybe sold out.

8. Eat proper meals, starting with breakfast (as Tessa advised) and eat sitting down at the table. Screen eating leads to overeating in my experience, whether it is laptop or telly.

9. Eat in public. I used to eat next to nothing in public. Frantically I would make up for it later in private. This was never a pretty sight.

10. Move your body in a way that suits you. For me it is yoga. I tried the gym, running, swimming, and found that all those activities increased my appetite and I ate more. Quite depressing to be swimming four miles a week and not losing any weight. Yoga works for me, and now I work at it.

11. Identify your saboteurs, and deal with then head on. These folks will subconsciously or otherwise try to feed you, with their pseudo cheery renditions of "go on, treat yourself." By the way these are without doubt the same people who criticized you for being fat. Learn the art of saying no and learn the art of eating for your own body and not to please others.

CHAPTER 3

PURA VIDA

"If all the year were playing holidays
To sport would be as tedious as to work."

Hal, from Henry IV Part One, Act 1, Scene 2

If anyone knows how to live happily it is Molly. At 13 years old she has the most stunning disposition, cheerful personality, and loving nature. Molly is such a kind and generous girl that at one point she spent her free time volunteering at a Toronto palliative care hospital. Molly's very presence at the hospital would help to lift the spirits of the patients, lighten their day, make them laugh and hopefully provide a few moments of joy. Before I paint an unrealistic and altogether too perfect picture of Miss Molly let me also confess that she possesses some unpleasant habits and behaviours. For example, Molly likes to hog the pillows, and can throw a death stare the length of a king sized bed if asked to share, or perish the thought, move. Molly snores more loudly than the passing ships can fog horn. Molly can be stubborn and although stone deaf still gives the impression of ignoring you when you know she can see you perfectly well and is fully aware of the exact meaning of the hand signals you are frantically waving in her direction. Without doubt, Molly's most vile habit is that she likes to eat cat shit in the garden. Molly is, of course, my dog, an English Cocker Spaniel. As a childfree adult she is my child substitute, not that I ever wanted to have children but I recognize maternal instincts when I feel them even if they are directed towards an English Cocker. I am unashamed in my joy at parenting a pup.

I read somewhere that you know your dog is a child substitute when you have more than two names for your pet and refer to your own parents as the pet's grandparents. Molly is also known as Molly Johnson (for the Toronto based Jazz singer after Molly's Father and I fell in love with each other and with Molly Johnson one evening at the Top of the Senator in December 1994); Mollerina; Mollerina Babcock; Babs; Babushka; Babinsk; Babaliscious; Lolly; Lolla; The Loll; Molybdenite (thanks to her cousins following a visit to the ROM minerals room when they were seven and four years old, with some help from their Mother I suspect); Molium (thank you Grandpa the medic); Molecule (smallest unit, thank you Grandma the *Guardian* Quick Crossword fan); and Molster, because after all, although she is, like her Mother, English, she is (also like her Mother) Canadian. Her official title is Victoriana Tea Time Surprise. That makes me think of Nigella Lawson, who officially holds the cards to call herself The Right Honourable Nigella Lawson but chooses not to. Molly is much the same. One of my friends Jerry, at the time we adopted Molly, suggested calling her "Surprise" so we could stand at the back door shouting "Surpri . . ."

Additionally, as Lovely Husband frequently enjoys pointing out, Molly does not borrow the car, does not bring home questionable boyfriends or poor report cards, and she *rarely* stomps off to her room yelling that she hates us, followed by a vicious slamming of doors. She did turn and face the wall once when Lovely Husband teased her by paying too much attention to Cherry Blossom or was it Mrs. Duck, I forget, but really who can blame her, one's toys are one's toys.

Molly is no longer a Pet Therapy Volunteer at the hospice, and I must be clear that this was not on my watch, but rather under her Father's kindness and direction. We now have shared custody of Molly and she is fortunate enough to have a city home and a country home and two families who love her. I confess shared custody is a godsend when it comes to travelling, but our house is not the same when she is absent from it. I miss the sound of those doggy toes clicking on the hardwood and the fact that wherever you are in the house Ms. Babcock is right there with you. Molly has three beds at our house, one on every floor. She enjoys walks, ear-rubs, biscuits and playtime on tap. When I die I plan to come back as Molly.

I have lost two beloved friends to cancer. The first was Mary. Dr. Mary was my friend from 1994 until she died in New Zealand, long before her time, in March 2006. Upon the last occasion I spoke to Mary which was February 23 that year, I knew during our phone call that unless I jumped on a plane, soon, I likely would not see her again. Lovely Husband and I immediately planned a nine-day trip to New Zealand departing in a couple of weeks. We didn't make it, and neither did Mary. We gave the cost of one airfare to the NZ Cancer Society in Mary's name, and later in the year my parents bought me a euonymus alatus, which we planted at the end of the garden and is only ever referred to as The Mary Tree. As I write this it feels like an untruth as in a "Mary's dead? Don't be ridiculous, you just haven't heard from her in a while" sort of way. When someone lives in another country and dies and you don't make it to the funeral, it is all rather surreal. I understand now why funerals are for the living.

Mary was a smart, bright, clever woman, a bluestocking as my Granny would have said, earning her PhD in her early forties after a successful career in the public sector. Mary became a well-known and respected academic with an enviable publishing record, which intensified and magnified after moving from the UK to New

Zealand in the late nineties, where she held distinguished academic positions. Mary was a true intellect in a way that I know I could never be and I admired her enormously for that alone. Mary was a lover of fine white wine (she lived in New Zealand after all), sexy shoes, good haircuts (and colour), clothes in general, books, dancing, and travel. Mary was first and foremost a traveller. She once told me that her nieces used to point at planes, look at their Mother and say "Auntie Mary." I actually borrowed that story a few times and have been known to pass it off as my own thinking it made me sound glamorous and worldly. Mary would find that amusing, and no doubt encourage me to keep it.

At least once a year Mary would sweep through the USA as New Zealand academics are (or at least were then) given plenty of opportunity and funds to travel, attend conferences and speak. Without such travel privileges I suspect the universities realized they would lose their hard won talent to overseas institutions. One of the many things I learned from Mary is that regardless of the circumstances there is always enough money for travelling. As a result, whether I could afford it or not (often not), I would meet Mary wherever she happened to be in the USA for an Academy of Management Conference or similar. We met in Chicago, New York City, San Diego, Washington DC, and LA with a road trip to Santa Barbara in a Mustang convertible, all very Thelma and Louise. I used to do the driving. Mary would always want to drive for just a few miles, to prove that she could and say that she had. In truth she was a lousy driver, even to the point of being stopped by the California Highway Patrol for rolling through a stop sign in La Jolla. She blustered her way out of a ticket through excessive flirting and an exaggerated use of the English accent, but shortly thereafter I became the designated Thelma. When we both still lived in the UK we spoke (separately) at the same conference in Minneapolis and afterwards hired a white Dodge Neon and drove up to Duluth for a night, along Lake Superior, and over into Canada just for the fun of it. We ate pancakes in Pigeon River, Ontario and then drove back. It was March and we were equipped with a bottle of water, a bag of pretzels and a novel each. Natural-outdoorsy-survivor-types that we were.

Now that I no longer have Mary, I cannot tell you how grateful I am to have shared those adventures. I never fail to laugh out loud at the photograph I took of Mary surreptitiously shaking off a pair of flat sandals in Tijuana, Mexico and sliding into a set of killer heels (which matched her dress) all for the sake of the photo (she had a duff knee at the time and had been placed on a strict sensible shoe diet). A complex and fascinating woman, Mary was scared of dogs but pursued an African safari unable to explain how Fido was a fright but the Big Five were fine. Mary would steadfastly refuse to do anything she did not want to do but would never prevent you from going ahead, saying with her mischievous grin and lightening eyes, "no thanks, but I'll hold your coat." Mary watched her weight carefully, ate healthily (mostly vegetarian), and followed a regular exercise regime. In fact she had started to compete in triathlons before she became ill and would celebrate at the finish line with a turkey sausage. She died of colon cancer at the age of 48. I miss Mary, and as we often said to each other, usually as we were standing nervously and twitchily in airport departure lounges awaiting flights back to our adopted countries, "I miss me when I am not with you." Sadly and perhaps predictably, I have lost touch with Mary's husband John, fine chap that he was. I hope he is happy in his corner of the world.

The second beloved friend I lost to cancer was a John himself. John Dewhurst, only child of Elsie and Harold Dewhurst of Blackburn, Lancashire. The Dewhursts lived at 66 Colenso Road and had been neighbours to my Mother when she was a child. My Mother, Ann, lost her own Mother, Louisa, when Ann was only five years old. Aunty Elsie and Uncle Harold became surrogate parents to little Ann Brown and in turn surrogate grandparents to My Sister and to me. I don't think I have ever had a fan as big as Aunty Elsie, nor will again. I would stay at 66 Colenso Road for a week or so during the summer holidays when I was a child and literally weep when it was time to go home. My Mother must have been thrilled at the end of the those holidays as she arrived to collect her ungrateful offspring.

Aunty Elsie was a fabulous dresser, Renata and Bally shoe snob, and a savvy businesswoman. In the early 1940s, with only 100 pounds sterling, Elsie Dewhurst (nee Wroe) opened *Elsie Wroe* the exclusive ladies gown shop which she ran successfully for many years while looking after an invalid Mother, young Ann Brown, a fox terrier called Thimble, and, for a few years dodging the air raids while separated from her husband Harold who was god-knows-where on the convoys, and still she managed to do the buying for her shop 200 miles away in London. The Aunty Elsies were the silent heroines of their generation. Aunty Elsie was also a lady mason (which was a big deal in those days), and a true blue Tory, just right of Margaret Thatcher we used to say, who was utterly convinced that the Queen voted Conservative. Elsie Dewhurst was a loyal and doting Mother and Grandmother to her children and grandchildren, real and adopted, and by the way, a terrible cook famous for her nineteen-minute steaks, and peculiar orange tarragon chicken, which was something of a signature dish in the Dewhurst household. If I even whisper "orange tarragon chicken" to My Sister now we are each uncontrollable for a full five minutes. Admittedly Aunty Elsie did make the best sherry trifle west of the Pennines, score one for the puddings.

And what of Uncle Harold? Well, he was the last of a dying breed of English gentlemen, the likes of which we shall not see again. I last spoke to him on my 18th birthday when he called me from Australia while visiting his son John. When Aunty Elsie returned from that trip and we met her at Manchester airport, she was all alone, with tormented eyes, hollow cheeks, and wearing Harold's watch on her slender wrist.

From the Lake Blog January 4, 2011: Like a Kiss without the Squeeze

> *My lovely Uncle Harold from Lancashire, England, and alas long gone, used to say that "apple pie without the cheese is like a kiss without the squeeze." Lancashire Crumbly cheese of course. I always loved that expression and am applying it to the time of year ripe for resolutions, the early days of January. Ah the resolutions we will make and the promises, mostly to ourselves, we will break. So if apple pie without the cheese is like a kiss without the squeeze then a resolution without a Plan is like a river without a dam. The ideas will flow and the images are rapid, exciting and full of energy and potential. Unless we harness that potential and contain that energy it will simply move on, without us. The dam, or rather the Plan, will hold the energy, shape the idea and provide a tangible outcome. So this year, have a slice of Plan with your resolutions, set milestones, celebrate the wins, and above all implement, implement, implement.*

Elsie and Harold's son, John Wroe Dewhurst moved to Australia, from the UK, in the late 70s as a trained clinical psychologist, fell in love with the country and a woman, had three boys, and never came back to live in the UK. Patterns emerge in all families I suspect. Looking ahead I would put money on my niece Hannah living overseas, but that is for another day. John, another avid traveler, did make it to Canada twice. Once in 2007 for a visit as part of a larger North American and European tour, and again in June 2008 for our wedding. John too had colon cancer and kept himself focused throughout his illness by buying plane tickets and planning his next big trip. How lucky we were to have seen him twice in two years. Before that I had not seen him since October 1999 when we met in the UK for the sad occasion of Aunty Elsie's funeral. There is nothing so grim as taking a flight for a funeral. John called our house one Sunday morning in April 2009 from Australia to say his goodbyes and died four days later. I answered the phone that morning.

The joy of a dog and the death of friends are gentle and harsh reminders respectively to live well. "Eat, drink and be Mary" as we used to say. I lost another friend in 2009, I seem to be at an age when people are dying, and on the way home from Mike Perrin's funeral I pulled off the QEW and had a bloody good cry. I lost a contact lens in the process and had to complete the rest of the drive with one eye closed. I had seen my ex husband at this funeral, and many people from our earlier days together in Toronto as this friendship was from my former life. Although I certainly cried at the wastefulness of the world in being so careless at to let a man as good as Mike Perrin go before he had a chance to turn 50, I also cried for me, selfish as that sounds, recognizing that if I died now I would feel so absolutely fucking cheated. I realized I hadn't done enough with my life, was wasting much of it stuck in a job I no longer wanted and complaining so frequently that I was tired of hearing myself think never mind speak. It was high time, long overdue, and way past its sell by date that I made significant changes and get on with the second half of my life. Yes, and even admit that I am now in middle age and likely not going to be randomly selected by a movie scout while strolling through the Eaton Centre at lunchtime. In fact the only occasion on which I am randomly selected is at airports. With a name like Rashmi Biswas, and being in possession of an appearance that is indeterminate in origin, I make for an easy target.

When I received my Canadian passport in the mail in early March 2010 Lovely Husband and I were swift to try it out by crossing into upstate New York one evening for dinner. As we approached the border booths I began to have slight anxiety that my freshly minted Canadian passport would not be accepted and that this excursion may not go well after all. Forgive my skepticism but my previous experiences of entering the US whether at the Peace Bridge, Rainbow Bridge, or through YYZ since 9/11 have all been rather unpleasant affairs involving lengthy questions, being pulled out of lines (randomly) finger-printed, retina photographed, and that of all round general humiliation. On one memorable occasion en route to Puerto Rico I would have cheerfully (make that tearfully) turned back and stayed in Toronto had it not been a business trip on which I was accompanying Lovely Husband and could not let the side down, a definite chin up moment. On this March evening as we handed over the dark blue passports to Border Guy he looks at me and asks "Rashmi?" in a rather quizzical disbelieving tone. Here we go think I, turn the car around we are not going through this again, when said Border Guy continues, "Huh, Rashmi, beautiful name." Had I heard him correctly? Was this the extent of the questioning? Was Lovely Husband really putting the car in drive, buzzing up the window and proceeding towards I95? How odd that Rashmi in possession of a British passport was never in possession of a beautiful name. However, I should not be ungrateful, so I am not.

Moving on with a new life involves no regrets, and when required, a definite focus-forward-with-cut-price-tuna attitude.

Lovely Husband and I coined this phrase after receiving and paying not one, but two, spectacularly nasty and unexpected bills in March 2010, each within two weeks of the other. Whatever the change brings the side benefits are learnings, personal development and ultimately growth. Running head first into the future, coming ready or not.

From the Lake Blog May 24, 2010: Take The Hard Road

The creative process is a fascinating activity and hard to capture, measure, replicate or describe. Being creative as a team brings a unique set of challenges, and decisions have to be made on how to proceed. Work alone, and come up with draft ideas on paper and share them in two days time? Or, tough it out, real time, verbally, and in person, agree, don't agree, and use the confrontation, conflict and chaos with a blind faith that brilliance will strike, and the product will evolve and grow like a precocious child before our eyes. Working on a particular Planning model recently we adopted the latter approach, and, after a few terse words, long silences and half a packet of printer paper, we did indeed watch our model learn to ride its bike and go off to ballet classes while speaking French and playing the violin. There are parallels here between the training versus coaching argument. Training is a clean, almost clinical activity, in a climate-controlled environment, with carefully prepared materials on crisp white sheets waiting to be read and written upon. Training takes place in an ordered world of flipcharts, power point slides (with no spelling mistakes), deliciously smelly coloured pens, pastel post-it notes, and most importantly defined behavioural norms established for the instructor and the participants, and, by and large, adhered to by all involved. Coaching on the other hand is unscripted, unpredictable, unknown. If training is a well-directed movie with the badly delivered lines deleted and imperfect body parts airbrushed, then coaching is improv, with "before" photographs. Coaching is reality management. Train for skills by all means; train someone to learn how the accounting system works, train someone to use the phone system, however, coach someone to improve, coach someone to up-sell, coach someone to deliver exceptional customer service, and coach someone to reach their goals. Coaching is undoubtedly the harder road, yet it brings the best results.

As a trainer first and foremost I thoroughly enjoyed working as a people manager, recognizing it to be the toughest yet most rewarding part of the job. I know everyone says that as a classic corporate platitude and I often wondered, sometimes out loud to others, how anyone could handle a people manager's role without a Human Resource background. Perhaps they possess finer instincts than I. A few months after leaving my job as a Regional Manager, where I had led a team of 28 direct reports, I heard from a third party that during a recent meeting members of my former team had identified me as one of the people they considered to have had a positive impact upon them during their time with the company. I'm not bragging, well perhaps just a tad, and naturally I was deeply touched by this feedback, and even had a small cry. Far from feeling regretful or wistful that I should have remained in that position where I was valued and appreciated, I felt validated in having made the decision to leave. I suspect if I had remained in place for much longer, and perhaps begun to outstay my welcome, I likely would have ceased to inspire such confidence. Knowing when to leave is an important life skill.

When contemplating new possibilities, or considering a monumental shift, or grand move I am fascinated by the roadblocks we self-construct, serving only to halt and hinder our every forward movement. Self-constructing in order to self-destruct is a curious concept. It sometimes happens with me and food. If I am feeling especially slim and gorgeous for let's say a couple of weeks (hey, it happens) I then go on a breakaway re-familiarizing myself with all the *Dairy Milk* products known to woman and consequently set myself back 3lbs. Where does this urge to self-sabotage originate? Is it a fear of being successful or perhaps the fear of being noticed? Am I afraid to be slim? Or do I feel that having lost a few pounds I can afford a binge? Worryingly I fear it is a bit more complicated, stemming from a deep-rooted fear of failure, an emotion so strong that rather than fail one will not even compete?

In March 2010 Lovely Husband and I were fortunate to holiday in Costa Rica, booked I might add prior to the arrival of the evil twin demand letters, repeat the mantra "focus forward with cut price tuna." This trip was to be my second visit to Cost Rica and Lovely Husband's first. We enjoyed the people, the pineapple, the volcanoes, the charcoal coloured beaches, the greenest of rainforests, and most of all the dense jungle complete with seemingly on-demand wildlife. Lovely Husband and I share a pathological fear of heights and in fairly short order discussed and dismissed the idea of zip lining across the jungle canopy. When we first looked at condos together in Toronto one unwitting realtor took us to the 30 something floor of the Pantages building. As the clueless yet enthusiastic agent is ripping back the blinds to showcase the floor to ceiling window the length of the living room, with spectacular jump-now drop and view, Lovely Husband and I are plastered up against the back wall, sweat pouring from our brows, knees a-wobbling and stomachs a-churning. While in Costa Rica I thought about booking the zip line tour every day for two weeks, but could not bring myself to do it. Should have done it.

I once had a yoga teacher in Toronto who frequently pleaded with us to "get out of your own way." Working daily, striving and struggling to ensure Lake became a success and that I was able to make a living from it was a straightforward matter of getting out of my own way. The road ahead in self-employment is filled with red lights, roadblocks and detours. It is staggeringly easy to have a good idea one day only to shoot it between the eyes the next. The lack of regular income coupled with the expense of starting a business can certainly have one lying awake at night. I was paying myself out of my savings. The same savings in fact I had set aside for the PhD. Same difference really, it was for my future, and the future was now. Many times in 2010 I could be found in the kitchen at 3:22am with a mug of Earl Gray tea, pot lights dimmed, laptop screen glowing eerily in the dark, silently trawling Workopolis, searching and applying for proper jobs "just in case." Whenever I felt unbearably anxious, convinced that we would starve and I would ruin my career by staying away from the corporate world, I would engage in this Job Application Therapy late at night or early in the morning and I would be remedied for a little while longer. It was a safety net and occasionally I needed one. I needed to know that applying for jobs was always an option, and to see that there were jobs out there for which I was qualified and capable of performing. The Job Application Therapy lasted until I found myself getting halfway through an application for Director, Learning & Development with a financial company only to close it out, deliberately, without saving or sending. I did attend a couple of interviews and met some good people. In practice both the prospective employers and I knew that the job direction was not right for me. The rejection did not hurt or set me back, quite the opposite as I know now the cathartic benefits were in the process of searching and applying. The Job Application Therapy further reinforced that I already had the job I wanted. I certainly wasn't afraid of being successful this time. I was ready for success. As my former yoga teacher had insisted, it was indeed time to get out of my own way.

From the Lake Blog May 30, 2011: A True Competitor Achieves His Best

> *This inspiring note came to us from a friend who has been an active runner for a number of years. His goal was to deliver his best performance yet and in his own words describes how he achieved his plan. "I ran my first half marathon in October 2008 in approx. 2:08. At that point I set a personal goal of sub 2 hr. Prior to Sunday I had run three more with times of 2:00:15, 2:04 and 2:06. Each time I read more, I changed my plan; I worked hard but just couldn't achieve my goal. In January I made the decision to use a plan developed by Runners World and purchased a training program aimed directly at achieving a sub 2-hour time. I received daily emails for 14 weeks with a workout for the day, coaching tips and nutritional tips from the experts. Of course as of Sunday I exceeded my goal and attribute it all to them. It made me think of business planning and Lake and Associates. Sometimes no matter how you plan or how hard you work you still may not achieve your plan or discover your potential without good coaching from the experts." Best, Jim.*

CHAPTER 4

2010 THE YEAR OF THE SISTER

"Sisters is probably the most competitive relationship within the family, but once the sisters are grown, it becomes the strongest relationship."

Margaret Mead

My Sister is the kind of woman who should run for public office. I actually had this conversation with her recently and during our discussion we agreed that sadly, many good people no longer go into politics, no doubt for a host of reasons, not least because of the media spotlight, harsh treatment and inevitable personal scrutiny. Perhaps more off putting to the enthusiastic wannabe MPs is the sheer enormity of the task at hand. Early idealists motivated at the front end to change the system fear limping across the finish line jaded and frustrated like so many who have gone before. Additionally My Sister and I frequently lament the male dominated, middle class, career-politician make-up of the political benches, on either side, front and back.

The thought process behind this criticism, apart from the obvious narrow focus, lack of social representation and general all round self-satisfied smugness that these boys carry by claiming to know what's best for the rest, is the serious question of how can you lead when you have never led? How can you know what will work when you never have? I have never subscribed to the real world concept, or supported the notion that some arenas, most notably perhaps in my experience, academia versus corporate, are any more or less realistic than others. Universities, hospitals, schools, and public sector departments all have goals, targets, performance expectations, quotas, scrutiny, and are ultimately answerable to someone albeit a Board, a Customer, a Shareholder a Parent or a Student. There are few, if any, positions within these organizations where one could hold a credible position of influence with little or no qualifications or training. Being President of the USA is arguably the biggest job in the world. Yet here is a case in point where the incumbent is not required to possess any specific qualifications, training or experience. Agreed, running for the US Presidency is perhaps the longest job interview in the history of recruitment but even the outcome of that process comes down to stamina, nerves of steel, an aligned media machine, millions of campaign dollars, the odd celebrity endorsement, and spin. None of these are reliable or valid. Reliability and validity, as any Human Resource professional worth their BlackBerry will tell you, form the basis of all respectable and trusted selection tools out there in the so called real world. If it isn't reliable and it isn't valid, you shouldn't be using it.

Overhauling the electoral selection process by establishing qualifications and specific criteria for elected officials almost sounds like a threat to democracy, which clearly I am not interested in destabilizing, as it can be fragile enough in some parts of the world. What I will say however is that I do believe, with every fibre of my being, that in order to represent the public you need some bloody idea as to who the public are. And better yet, be one of their ilk not considering *them* to be *them* at all. Aren't we all members of the great unwashed in some form or another? Who is the man on the Clapham omnibus anyway? Isn't he every man, woman, and spaniel, as we say in our house?

Women generally (and I am generalizing here, but then everybody generalizes) perform enormous acts of public service, largely undetected, underappreciated and under the radar. Typically these herculean efforts (notice I cannot find a female equivalent) are carried out at the community level, grass roots, and front-line, involving roll your sleeves up kind of work. Women, again generally speaking, are not in this for the glory of serving. There is precious little glory in sorting donated goods at the Oxfam shop, just ask my Mother who ran such a shop for fifteen years. Nor, I suspect, are the people involved in this work purely altruistic. Lovely Husband has an Aunt Natasha who, at the age of 83, volunteers her time by singing to the old people with her choir. Aunt Natasha does not do this for glory, she does this because she cares, and, as a widow of over ten years, it keeps her busy, and socially active, making her feel wanted and needed to boot, and indeed she is. The by-products are that she is contributing positively to the richness of her own life and to the lives of others. This is public service with private benefits. Nothing wrong with that, providing one approaches public service for private benefits with positive intentions, using it for good and not for evil.

"Nearly all men can stand adversity, but if you want to test a man's character, give him power."

Abraham Lincoln

There was a study reported in the Economist a few months ago about a group of behavioural scientists in the Netherlands and in the USA who, in the light, or rather in the shadow, of some rather shabby behaviour by public officials from nowhere in particular and seemingly everywhere in general, were conducting experiments to determine whether power corrupts, as goes the adage, or whether in fact corrupt people are attracted to power. Fascinating. (Economist, January 21, 2010).

As a family, we have always shared a passion for politics. One of us organized student protests, hunger strikes and sit-ins in India in his twenties, don't ask. Growing up, dinner table conversations in our house would often turn to politics and from an early age My Sister and I learned to firstly, have an opinion, secondly, back it up with more than emotions, and thirdly express it clearly. We were good at the first of these and reasonable at the third; two was sometimes a stretch and so our Father encouraged daily *Guardian* newspaper reading to provide a source of information. I became a card carrying member of the Labour party at the age of 19 although confess to being somewhat disappointed and disillusioned with the levels of discussion at the local meetings much of which was focused on the traffic lights at the bottom of Hardhorn Road. Not the revolution I was looking for, but of course deliciously unglamorous, and grassroots (right back at you). Since becoming a Canadian citizen I am card carrying once again and this time getting fully involved to the point of having joined the campaign team in support of a smart, bright, switched on woman candidate I know and respect. This is good work and I am happy to be doing it.

My Sister did not join a political party in her youth and has yet to run for office, nor is she likely to. Political line-ups are lesser for it. My Sister involved herself in community events from an early age and today is a magistrate, a hospice volunteer and a bereavement counselor and trainer. All unpaid, all inglorious, all front-line, and all hard work. This is precisely why My Sister should run for office. That and the fact that she has also held proper jobs, worked for a living, paid a mortgage, successfully raised two rather incredible children (for several years by herself) and generally is one of the people I admire most in the world.

My Sister and I have not always got along as sisters should or would like to. There is 2 years, 5 months and 2 days between us, which, at times, felt like a cultural and anthropological ocean apart. For years we were so unalike I questioned whether we would even be friends if we had met under different circumstances. We were close when we were small, not close growing up and seemed to find each other again in 2010 at the ages of 45 and 42 respectively. Not to misstate this, we have always had each other's back and been involved in each other's lives but 2010 was without doubt The Year of the Sister, My Sister.

I maybe the only person in the world who was grateful to the Ash Cloud that consumed half of Europe and impacted practically everyone alive when it swept into view in mid April 2010. My Sister and Clive (top man brother-in-law) visited Lovely Husband, Molly and me in early April for a week's holiday. The travelers who had spent a few days in California wine tasting and Alcatraz visiting, came to stay with us in Niagara, and ended their North American Tour in Washington DC before heading home to the UK. While the travelers were breakfasting at a café in Georgetown, and planning a tour of the Senate for later in the day, the Icelandic volcano made its mark and all flights going anywhere were cancelled, as you no doubt remember. After much phone calling, texting, and researching, My Sister discovered that their flight from DC to Heathrow was rescheduled for ten days hence. Lovely Husband and I were also in the USA at that time, although just over the border having lunch, still testing out that new blue passport, and looking back at Canada across the river. According to *Garmina,* our personified GPS, if we left Lewiston at that precise moment we could be at the White House by teatime. Beds were made, towels were clean, "come back to us" was the unanimous cry. And so, catching an outrageously expensive Air Canada flight out of Washington, they did just that. And we had the gift of another week together. In total we spent six weeks in each other's company in 2010 which when you work for a living and live on different continents is quite the achievement.

One of the greatest gifts I received from My Sister in 2010, apart from her time and some splendid Molton Brown *Heavenly Gingerlily* body wash, was a lesson in change. And by that I don't mean as in the *"Who Moved My Cheese"* change lessons genre, but life lessons in changing oneself. Lessons in being open, and a willingness to look at others, and self, through a different lens is what matters here. Being mindfully flexible, mature enough, and big enough to be able to make changes to self and one's view of the world. Lifelong learning has always been a motto of mine yet I think up to this point I had only ever applied this to work, skills and courses. I had not previously considered myself to be an holistic project in the pursuit of lifelong learning. It hadn't occurred to me that I might change the parts of my character that I was none too pleased with. Sure I had changed the body, and I have been known to colour my hair, however as for changing the *who I am* bit, well that was just not in view. This had not been an intentional oversight on my part because I thought I was already perfect and could not possibly be improved upon, far from it. Up until this year I basically had failed to recognize and realize the latent power that rested dormant within whereby I could simply become a better person by choice and by actively choosing to change.

*From the Lake Blog September 9, 2010: Or At Least Change
Your Part of It*

*This morning I heard the talented Johnny Reid sing "Today
I am Gonna Try and Change the World." Johnny Reid was
live on "Q" with Jian Ghomeshi, and I loved the story behind
the song as Johnny Reid explained he was sending his son off
to school one morning and told him to "go and change the
world." Are you going to change the world today, or at least
change your part of it? What can you do today that would make
a positive impact on your work, your clients, your colleagues,
your future? I am off now to change the world . . . . or, at least
my part of it.*

Years ago when I was in the process of finishing school and
embarking upon my journey into higher education, a friend sagely
advised "change was the price we paid for growth." I don't remember
specifically what prompted this comment although as a 19 year old
leaving home for the first time one can imagine the general air of
discussion and issues pertinent to me at that stage in my life.

Perhaps I have taken this change-for-growth exchange rather too
closely to heart over the years. The jobs, the moving, the array of
activities, were all of these in pursuit of growth? The right question
would be did I actually grow as a result of all the changes? I certainly
have, like everyone else I am sure, had a vast array of experiences,
lived, travelled, tried, failed, succeeded, loved and wandered. Yet I
wonder whether these situational, environmental, name-over-the-
door changes have succeeded in delivering growth? You see this
is where I have my doubts. I sometimes rewind the PVR of my
life and view for a moment the seriously organized satchel-packed-
on-Sunday-afternoon worry wart schoolgirl, fast forward to the

feisty rather opinionated teenager, and definitely skip through the ads of the know-it-all student, and wonder if I have changed at all. I still worry incessantly, bordering on Obsessive Compulsive behaviours such as checking and re-checking locked doors and recently unplugged and now cooling hair straightening irons. Bath towels must be dried with the labels hanging to the back, loo roll must hang forwards (I have been known to change this in other people's powder rooms, my apologies), tins of chickpeas and kidney beans must face forward in the kitchen cupboards, yes just like in "*Sleeping with the Enemy.*" If there is a traffic accident in my town, or a fire anywhere I have visited recently, I wonder and worry if perhaps somehow I caused it. I understand all of this is pretty much textbook (mild) OCD behaviour. I replay conversations endlessly trying to remember verbatim what I and the other person said and the precise tone and inflection with which we said it. I will then laboriously and anxiously search this discourse picking over each comment with the intensity and vigour of a forensic accountant faced with dodgy books, seeking out the clues, which lead inevitably and invariably to my own failings. I am on a tear hunting for flaws, errors and missteps and in particular where the receiver may have established grounds to misunderstand, misrepresent, or sue me for misleading them. I can be haunted for no apparent reason by something I said or did a hundred years ago that will pop into my brain on a seemingly perfectly glorious stress-free day and it will gnaw away at my nerves taking hold of my mood and essentially hijacking what should have been a delightful experience. I worry that if I don't worry something will go wrong. It is actually a wonder I find the time to get anything done.

My phobias focus upon fires, law suits and labels, although I am not sure what that means. Perhaps in a former life I was Howard Hughes, although given that I was born in '67 and HH died in

'76 this explanation is now looking somewhat improbable. Plus, germs are not actually my OCD expression of choice. Although, I do enjoy being clean, of course, and I do participate in significant hand washing and try to avoid public bathrooms (but doesn't everyone?) and not only because of their often-questionable loo paper presentation.

Last year I was quite unkind to odd numbers and treated them with undue harshness. I have noticed that so far in 2011 I am more accommodating to their unevenness. I sense this may be connected to the calendar year and will have to monitor 2012 with close attention to accurately establish a pattern. The number preferences generally apply to the volume control on my car radio, the thermostat (again car only, not house), and, like my young nephew Alex, when reading a book and deciding where to close and bookmark the page, chapters that end on even numbered pages being the ultimate reward. I usually display candles and the like in threes but that is simply a matter of good interior design taste, I read *Style at Home*. Others are better positioned to identify whether or not I am still horribly opinionated, I feel less so, but then I would wouldn't I? As for feisty, well I can be, but overall I declare I am a calmer version of my former self, although Lovely Husband may take issue with that.

In April 2010 My Sister and I had long, frank discussions about my and her OCDness. Neither fully aware before this point that the other engaged in the same habits. This is not a particular burden to either one of us so I won't create a melodrama by saying this is an illness or disease we share or that we are joined in our pain. Our sharing of it however was important. Our newfound openness and candor succeeded in bringing us closer. By admitting, confessing and laughing, without judgment or cruelty, at our sometimes unique, sometimes individual and often combined quirks and flaws, we liked each other all the more.

I think in the past I had always put on rather a show when it came to My Sister. Not unlike stealing Mary's stories or pretending to be a great intellectual heavyweight. Far from being a Sister I had been an imposter. No wonder she didn't like me very much, my behaviour wasn't terribly likeable and more importantly it wasn't even me. I was acting the role of this Sister and person I thought I was supposed to be, or rather how I thought I wanted to see myself. The biggest laugh is on me at the end of this as the person I really am is the person my Sister can relate to, and vice versa, and this is the person who makes My Sister feel like she has a Sister too, a Sister who is genuine, unafraid to reveal the pluses and the minuses and willing to let another person truly get to know her. Finally, I had come down off my high horse and fortunately found My Sister waiting for me with open arms.

The personal renovation project that is supposed to take place when your passport pages fill with stamps or the job titles sound grander is a fake. I was the same person whatever destination was printed on the airline ticket or corporate badge appeared on my business card. Some friends reported that I had taken up all the space under "B" in their address books. I had lived in the same house as a child from the age of one to the age of 19 and have not stood still since. In Manchester I held three addresses, one in halls of residence, a shared terraced house next door to my future niece and nephew's future father, and finally a frigid flat on the top floor of a grand-in-its-day Victorian villa. Two places in Scotland, which was appallingly bad timing for me, a student at the time, as the Tories were road testing the Poll Tax that year and it was introduced north of the border before the rest of the country and therefore I had to cough up. One mews house in Surrey, which came rent-free for a year. Six addresses in Sheffield where I was burgled, moved with boyfriends, lodged with the wonderful Maria and on another occasion with the lovely Toby, and eventually learned to find peace in learning to live alone. One flat in Middlesbrough, again living alone, this time in a quaint market town, and one cottage in Northallerton, with another boyfriend and a fireplace that was too much work to light and clean so with not even a pub in the village (what were we thinking) we would shiver off to bed at 8:30pm every night. Four places in Toronto, an apartment at Yonge & Bloor, two houses in Bloor West (Upper Bloor West actually if you listen to the realtor speak) and a condo in the Beach (note that is Beach singular for those who have ever or currently do live there). The condo was right on Queen Street East opposite *Meat on the Beach,* and within spitting distance of a bookstore (where I once ran into and spoke to the delightful Heather Mallick) and a yoga studio, all of which adds up to my idea of heaven. Finally, for now, the current resting place is one grown-up house in Niagara with ships instead of fairies at the bottom of the garden. This is a total of 19 addresses in as many years, without I might add, joining the Army. I know I shall have to move again if only to make it an even number . . . . hmmmm, I rather regret adding all that up now.

I did in fact apply to join the Army as a teenager. I went to Preston, home of the Queen's Lancashire Regiment, and also to Donnington, which I can only recall as being the home of the Ministry of Defence. I visited these fine towns for the series of military medicals and military career interviews. I had a lovely army careers liaison officer called Captain Moorhouse or was it Moorehouse? I may have been a little bit in love with Cpt. M, not entirely sure, but I certainly idolized her and wanted to be her. HR types would secretly consider this to be an excellent recruitment tactic on the army's part, but would not admit it out loud. I even spent a couple of days, during the summer of 1986, in Guildford, Surrey, attempting to pass the "Pre-RCB" which consisted of a series of mental and physical tests, all this instead of going on holiday to Tenerife with my mates which is what most people did upon receiving their A-level results and before they headed off to university. I actually did pass the "Pre-RCB" that summer which was no mean feat for someone who at the time was only slightly fitter and faster than your average indoor cat. Admittedly I progressed to the next round with a sound warning delivered in a terribly posh voice from the bossiest of bossy selection board women to "B*e fit dear*" before the next round in the selection process. Right, yes, I will indeed Be Fit Dear. Shortly thereafter I went off to Manchester Polytechnic, discovered the joys of lying in bed, eating late night burgers, and watching all the telly I could handle, occasionally all at the same time, and never looked back, or for that matter, got fit, dear.

Arnold School Blackpool where my Sister and I completed our aged 11-18 education (studying for O-levels and A-levels as they were called then) was one of those schools where at the age of 14 you were forced to sign up for some version of cadets in the intra-institution known as the Combined Cadet Force or CCF. The blatantly uncool kids joined the navy, the counter culture see-how-cool-I-am-I-joined-the-air-force kids did just that, and the rest of us, who thought we were cool but weren't because we were following the pack like little lambs in black berets, joined the army. I joined the army. Baaahh.

My Sister, two years ahead of me, had joined the army, although she was a pukka cool kid. In practice My Sister spent every moment of her short-lived military career (two years and out) dreaming up creative applications of asthma afflictions as an excuse to extricate herself from pretty much anything army related, including walking, which is ironic considering she achieved her Duke of Edinburgh Bronze, Silver and Gold Awards without appearing to break a sweat. I *stayed on* in the Combined Cadet Force for two more years beyond the mandatory two and was promoted to the lofty rank of RSM (Regimental Sergeant Major) for my loyalty and more importantly I enjoyed the privilege of wearing a sludge green skirt for Friday afternoon appearances on the parade ground instead of the completely awful "yes sorry love your bum does look humungous in those DPMs." There is apparently no Distorted Pattern Material alive which is capable of camouflaging a large bottom. Interestingly my last corporate job title was RSM. This cannot be full circle?

All this moving should make me an excellent packer and picture hanger, when in reality I am not terribly good at either. I have paid the price for change, and certainly paid the Post Office for change of address privileges, but I admit to falling a bit shy when it comes to being rewarded with the growth bit. My self-assembly futon was missing an Allen key. Frankly I felt rather cheated. My cha-cha-cha-changes (with a nod to David Bowie), job changes that is, had delivered increased income. I have never earned lots of money but as one generally discovers, the salary improved as the jobs got worse. Actually the higher paying jobs were the toughest, which is perhaps no great surprise to anyone who has ever held one.

The low paying jobs, and there have been a few of those, were tough for different reasons. At the age of 14 I worked on a pig farm every Saturday morning. Actually it wasn't a real job as I was working for free, and the farm was doing me a favour in allowing me to be there at all. During the I-want-to-be-a-vet years I decided to pursue Animal Husbandry as part of my Duke of Edinburgh Award effort. Unlike My Sister I stopped at bronze. I simply couldn't read a map in a hailstorm if my life depended upon it, and nor for any reason I could think of did I care to learn. Older Sister pursues Duke of Edinburgh Award and drops CCF so younger sister takes the alternate path is likely the answer to this great mystery. To this day I am unable to smell wet canvas without freezing with fear rooted to the spot in the quaking dread that I am about to be yelled at by an overzealous geography teacher dressed up as a weekend warrior Robert Scott. Fortunately as a grown-up woman living in a house and in possession of a king sized bed I am rarely exposed to the scent of damp tent but it can happen. My passion for studying Animal Husbandry was driven by a love of all animals, although dogs and horses fought for top spot, and naturally the desire to become a vet when I grew up. Sadly my dreams of veterinary medicine were shattered after a rather direct discussion my Mother had at a parent teacher night with my then chemistry teacher, Charles Manson (I kid you not, although the man was a diamond). Mr. Manson advised Mother I would need straight As in all three sciences and to be able to lift a cow. We all agreed I would look elsewhere for professional fulfillment, although I secretly know I could have handled the heavy lifting bit.

While working on the pig farm my responsibilities included feeding the pregnant sows, who would chase all intruders to their pen viciously, causing me to fall and bang my head on more than one occasion; administering injections to newborn piglets (a few ccs of something to stave off infection into each butt cheek, I confess I cannot remember ever knowing exactly what the drug concoction consisted of but I was only 14 and quite good at doing as I was told); playing with the puppy-like weaners; watching the miracle of birth and pretending I was instrumental to the outcome; and of course literally shoveling shit. There is a life lesson in case you were looking for one, the miracle of life happens without your help and assistance but the poo clean-up is where your skills are required. Grab a shovel.

I enjoyed Saturdays with the swine, having always wished as a child that I had grown up on farm instead of in a three-bedroom semi on a main road. This dream would infuriate my Mother to no end when I callously expressed my fantasy aloud, which I did with some regularity for a number of years. Mother in turn would accuse me of being ungrateful. It was, upon reflection, a fair and well matched exchange and to seal the deal Mother made me undress in the garden when I returned home from the pig farm for lunch, and I, rebelliously, stopped eating bacon.

My Sister had much more sensible and glamorous Saturday employment such as working in a shoe shop. I had thought this was glamorous work until My Sister informed me that dealing with feet all day, particularly feet that had spent the best part of the day carrying an overweight holiday-maker up and down the Golden Mile, often in the rain, was not the most appealing of jobs. I believe her.

As kids we would play shop when we went to visit our Gran, who was really our Step Gran but that doesn't matter. We would commandeer a bed sheet or tablecloth and create a storefront using a couple of upturned dining chairs in the back room of the terraced house on Winston Road. The playing bit typically involved dragging all the canned and dried goods out of Gran's pantry, arranging and displaying them for a few minutes and then the moment boredom struck, transferring them all back again. I expect it took our Gran weeks to find the cocoa and carnation milk after we had been to visit.

CHAPTER 5

LOOKING UP

"Tell me who admires and loves you,
And I will tell you who you are."

Charles Augustin Sainte-Beuve

I certainly admire My Sister, other members of my family and of course my friends. When asked to name my heroes, however, I have often struggled to come up with even one random name while others seemed perfectly capable of rattling off platoons of idols, gushing with excitement, and listing the reasons why this author or that athlete has inspired them. This ability to love and admire total strangers had always eluded me.

Failing to freely admire those I did not know was further weakened by my failure to even acknowledge that I admired the *talents* of those whom I did not know, yet others revered. I recall a rather terse discussion I had with Lovely Husband when watching Michael Phelps swim to eight gold medal victories at the Birds Nest stadium in Beijing during the summer of 2008. Lovely Husband declared Michael Phelps to be a hero, and I, grouchy, bitter, and thoroughly unpleasant, grumbled that the lad was just a swimmer and I admired the working mothers who got up at 5am everyday, ran busy households while holding down a full time job and still barely made ends meet. What I was really saying of course is that

I am disappointed with my own lack of success and am jealous of those who have succeeded.

I have never been one to take the populist view and rather prided myself on this.

Oh you write poetry,
Ooo you must be strange.
It's not me that smokes twenty,
I'm not deranged.

Rashmi Biswas, 1983

Writing poetry was not a particularly strong point for me. It was a passion for a while but evidently not a gift. I did spend many a Friday night home alone with a typewriter churning out maudlin musings, and yes my parents did worry about me.

I affectionately look back to this fiercely unpopular behaviour, and off the wall distinctly un-mainstream views, that I and your average sixteen year old would hold, and one of these days I want to read a few of my pitiful poems (if I can find the rest of them) at an open mike session in Toronto where we fortysomethings read extracts from our childhood literary efforts. I love it, it's definitely so bad it's good and distinctly refreshing and therapeutic to laugh at one's self. Judging from the above anti-smoking stanza there wasn't much laughing at one's self going on with me in the early eighties.

Learning to not take everything, well life really, quite so seriously and not being envious or snobbishly insufferable, became a new endeavour of mine in 2010. Let Mike Phelps be someone's hero, why not? And with that in mind I watched the Vancouver Olympics earlier in the year with a new found balance and pride, in spite of not being even remotely a fan of watching any sport on television, which further proves my alienation from much of the world, including I might add, on this topic, every member of my own family bar, Lovely Husband.

I understand (now) that people need someone to look up to, opportunities and dreams to cling to, in a that-too-could-be-me kind of way. Or better yet, simply because we are capable of seeing and admiring the positive in another person. This was a new concept or more accurately, a fresh perspective, and I was pretty excited to explore it further.

From the Lake Blog October 1, 2010: I Miss Freddie Mercury

> *It was announced last week that Sacha Baron Cohen would play the role of Freddie Mercury in an upcoming movie about the band Queen. As a life-long Queen fan, and Freddie devotee, I welcome the news, not only about SBC whom I believe will do an excellent job, but also to learn that there will be a Queen movie, as I do indeed miss Freddie Mercury . . . I pulled out my DVD of the 1986 "Live At Wembley" concert and once again am reminded and floored by Freddie's ability to lead the crowd and engage the fans . . . this is leadership in action. Take a look at "Radio Ga Ga" and watch in awe as the audience synchronize every move, clap and wave. Why do they do this? That's easy, because they want to, because Freddie makes them want to.*

Following the sporting example, I understand how sharing a love of the game connects people. During the World Cup Soccer (football) in South Africa, I would text and email my niece and My Sister regarding the goals, the results, or sometimes just to complain that those bloody vuvuzelas were getting on my nerves, which they did. I couldn't have cared less about the footie but it kept us close at 3000 miles apart.

True admiration for a person you are not intimate with is a test of character, imagination and generous spirit. If we are too consumed by our own limitations, and in a firm and perhaps overpowering possession of a keen sense of our own failings, we will never be able to see the good in others. We are blinded to the positive simply because we are overwhelmed by our own crippling negative. Human nature, likely as not, cannot help but admire another's success, without comparing this success (however you measure it) to her own, and in doing so will surely find herself to be lacking. Is this in fact a gender issue? I have long subscribed to the equally long standing belief that when applying for jobs, women who possess nine out of the ten requirements will refrain from submitting an application because they consider themselves to be inadequately qualified. Men, on the other hand who are in possession of say three out of the ten attributes then consider themselves to be ideally suited and of course apply for the position before you can say "hit send." Tiresome as it can be to reduce everything to a dichotomy between the sexes the examples do tend to reveal themselves with startling regularity. I have frequently been accused of looking for gender issues everywhere, and the response to that is easy, it is because they are everywhere. I am saddened by the lack of feminist progress as we glide into the second decade of the twenty first century and I am, at the risk of sounding dramatic, totally horrified at the sexualization of young women in these times. A staggering number of girls of school-leaving age, if the surveys are to be believed, set their career sights on becoming models, reality TV stars, lottery winners, or the wife of some famous rich guy. The objectifying of women continues and I continue to be disappointed by the credible actresses of my own age, and younger, who feel the need to bare all in order to make it on to the latest cover of Sexist Weekly or should that be *Weakly* because really my friends you are not doing the movement any favours here. Would these same women have us believe their nakedness and sexuality is empowering and that they are being ironic and having the last laugh when the cheques come in? Good luck with that as I believe it is what's known as winning the battle and losing the war.

With sex trafficking in Europe, Asia, and frankly the world, at an all time high, with the use of rape a commonplace weapon during wars across the globe, with women's shelters bursting at the seams in our local cities, when Haitian camps are filled with unwanted babies after their mothers have been systematically abused and raped while the authorities stand by all but helpless, when women are being stoned to death upon the instruction of those in charge, and while the debates surrounding abortion continue to permeate seemingly every political dialogue and election campaign in North America, it certainly feels as though we have a long way to go. If we want to end the violence against women, and I know we all do, then we need to devalue the currency of women's sexuality. Objectifying can only result in dehumanizing, which means I can pretty much do what I want with or to you because I am a person of importance and you are not. Simple. Terrifying, but simple.

I am sorry to admit I know some men who are wretchedly sexist, openly using disparaging language and tone, and displaying negative attitudes towards women on a seemingly daily basis. This is executed with such ease and subtlety that I suspect these men remain blissfully unaware of the impact of their actions. Many of these men have daughters and would no doubt consider themselves to be right-on-lefty-feminist types. As we say in Organizational Development speak if you want to change the culture change the language. I read recently that Oprah has banned the word b*tch from her new OWN network, bravo Ms. Winfrey, this is a bloody good start.

The gender imbalance and bias is so pervasive that unbelievably it is becoming less acceptable to speak out, and as women we are even doing this to ourselves. Women occasionally play up to the chaps to win short-term high-priced favour by trading on the reputations of other women. Sisterhood must be lived and practiced yet the tragedy is that all too often women commit this kind of gender traitor behaviour by betraying each other, in public, and on an ongoing basis. While watching the 83rd Academy Awards the other night and simultaneously following the much more interesting chat on Twitter about the show I was stunned by the negative comments and criticisms women were making about the appearances of other women. And I follow a number of women-with-a-cause type tweeters. I have made a promise to myself, and to my gender, that no more will I comment negatively about another woman, at all if I can help it, and definitely never to score points. If I criticize her then I criticize me, and I convey the notion to anyone within earshot that both are perfectly acceptable. I am self-deprecating but I am not a fool.

I missed the precise moment at which everything become so pink. It appears to have seeped into the consciousness like a sickly sweet dessert you wish you had resisted the moment the last forkful passes your lips. Have Benjamin Moore secretly been stockpiling oceans of the stuff keeping it out of sight in the 70s, 80s and 90s only to launch it upon the world in all its garish nausea in spring 2005?

I applaud the folks at Pink Stinks http://www.pinkstinks. co.uk/ and support them in their quest to highlight and promote positive role models for girls and young women. Not since the fifties have we been so bombarded with the apparently physical ideals of women's weight, shape, age, and clothing. Blaming telly and the media in general is hardly an original thought but given that all this discussion has failed to improve the status quo I am having my rant. Why in TV commercials when woman are fronting the sale of a product must the actress be dressed in the same colour as said product? For example, if the air freshener is baby blue then so is her sweater. Women? Objects? Don't get me started. And who, I want to know, is watching all these badly written, unfunny, base humour sit-coms where the main character is an ordinary looking buffonic bumbling man with a clever save-the-day-knock-out wife, and yet unfathomably he is the star. And really, *Cougar Town*? Is this the level to which we have sunk? Yet I know a number of women who think this show is hilarious and take no offense from the title. The turkeys are voting for Christmas, love a duck.

We have regressed into becoming girly girls even at the grand ages of middle years and beyond. A night out with the girls; girls getaways; referring to your all female staff as my girls; good grief what century are we in, and what messages are we sending? I promise to make an example of the next person who refers to me as a girl or worse addresses me in the collective "Hello Ladies" when sending a work related email to a group of professional women. Frankly it is up to me to set them straight after all silence is consent. The power is ours to do something and essentially we are throwing it away for a cheap laugh and a love me in the moment comfort zone. How many women do you know who play down their own intelligence to be sure they don't outshine their dull spouse? Can we just say I am going out with my friends tonight? Could we simply call our teams our teams? Can we please choose to disagree with our men folk in public without them feeling as if they have been castrated and paraded naked around the village square?

The women a few generations ahead of us, some of whom I know well such as the wonderful Maria, who paved the way for generations of women to come, by speaking out and in turn created pressure for Equality, achieved Equal Pay legislation, secured women's rights to access higher education, fought for paid maternity leave and of course even further back secured the vote, all must be tragically disappointed in us. We, the women of the twenty first century, who, with every opportunity available and door cracked at least slightly open, have opted to throw it all away in favour of marrying a footballer and buying an "It Bag."

"Well-behaved women rarely make history."

Laurel Thatcher Ulrich

If we do nothing else we can educate our girls. Some may still choose to marry well rather than work for a living, or make a living by uncovering their bodies for trash magazine covers. I am however more optimistic than perhaps I sound, and I do know smart bright young women who illustrate the point. And they give me hope. I have faith that many young women will become inspired when they learn about some of the amazing women in all areas of the world, becoming forces to be reckoned with in a range of arenas be it business, politics, arts, education or science, and decide that perhaps they too want to be Marissa Mayer (Google) Indra Nooyi (Pepsi), Lisa Lisson (FedEx), Bonnie Brooks (The Bay), Laura Chinchilla (Costa Rica) when they grow up. Or perhaps they will decide to be themselves, and spend time figuring out who that woman is, and then spend time being her, and being true to themselves.

A couple of weeks ago Lovely Husband and I watched "*Nowhere Boy*" the fabulous Sam Taylor-Wood movie about John Lennon's teen years. The movie portrays a young John absolutely transfixed while watching a not-much-older-than-John Elvis perform. Elvis is shown not only introducing a whole new sound to an entire generation but he is seen commanding and mesmerizing the audience in the process, for my generation this was the Freddie Mercury factor in action. At that precise moment in his life it appears young Lennon decides his own fate. It matters not what we choose, so long as there are choices to be had and positive role models to consider. Naturally as it turns out JL made a pretty wise decision.

And finally, to the "*Toddlers and Tiaras*" mothers and fathers dressing their five year olds, and younger, in revealing outfits, accompanied by hair, nails and make-up that would not look out of place among the cast of "*Priscilla*" please, we implore you to give your heads a shake. Your girls are still girls, and they need you.

Five Days from the Food Diary

<u>May 27—weight 135lbs—60 minutes yoga</u>

- All Bran, muesli, milk, blueberries, 6 grapes
- Half tin of chickpeas, carrots, cherry toms
- 2 x sausages, half tin of baked beans
- 2 glasses of wine, almonds
- 2 x teaspoons peanut butter
- Slice cherry pie

<u>May 28—weight 138lbs—30 minutes elliptical (cherry pie induced guilt)</u>

- All Bran, muesli, milk, blueberries, 6 grapes
- 1 x tin tuna, 3 x baby beetroot, carrots, 1 x teaspoon mayo
- Green curry chicken, 1 x tablespoon rice
- 2 glasses of wine
- 2 x teaspoons peanut butter

<u>May 29—weight 136lbs</u>

- Oatmeal, blueberries, milk
- 1 x tin tuna, 1 x teaspoon mayo, spring onion, beetroot, cherry toms, carrots
- Chicken breast, cauliflower, peas, onion, mushrooms
- 2 glasses of wine, 20 almonds
- Half cup frozen yoghurt

<u>May 30—weight 136lbs—75 minutes yoga</u>

- Oatmeal, blueberries, milk
- 2 x sausages, half tin baked beans
- 2 glasses of wine
- Half cup frozen yoghurt, 1 x teaspoon peanut butter

<u>May 31—weight 135lbs—60 minutes yoga</u>

- Oatmeal, blueberries, milk
- Carrots, cherry toms, cauliflower, almonds
- Dahl, chicken curry
- 2 glasses wine
- Half cup frozen yoghurt
- 2 x teaspoon peanut butter

From the Lake Blog October 26, 2010: What Am I Bringing to the Party?

I tweeted about this earlier today but I think it is worthy of a blog. I have observed and appreciated some super positive customer service experiences lately, including Rogers on-line support, Mercatto restaurant in Toronto, and by George clothing store in St. Catharines. The common ground is how friendly the staff was and therefore in response I was also friendly. The results were upbeat, positive and enjoyable interactions. Who knew that calling for BlackBerry service support on a Sunday afternoon could be a pleasant experience, well, honestly, it was, thanks to the person at the other end of the phone. Cause and effect perhaps. Absolutely. The social sciences and anthropologists talk about Reflexivity, where a researcher's very presence impacts a situation or dynamic. As a leader, customer service provider, manager or sales professional, what are you bringing to the party?

Deciding to categorically change one's attitude, and recognizing the capability within one's "You Resources" to do so, is indeed a life enhancing opportunity. My a-ha moment did not arrive as a result of being trapped alone on a mountain for three days, nor had I experienced any form of near death encounter, although I did choke on a piece of beef over dinner one evening in October and Lovely Husband seconds away from calling 911 performed the Heimlich maneuver with immediate success. I hadn't lost a parent or given birth to quads at the age of 41. My moment emerged in a decidedly more subtle fashion, with little in the way of fanfare and a great deal of stealth. My moment crept up on me over a period of a year, more or less, as a result of letting go. I consciously let go of years of holding on to false beliefs about myself. In remaining acutely aware that I was letting go I was able to pay close attention to the present. The most significant shift was in giving myself permission. Permission to look after myself and permission to not give a shit about how it looked to anyone else. Perhaps a serial pleaser in the past, in 2010 I actually took care of myself. And it is true what the flight attendants tell you on take-off, you cannot help another with their oxygen mask until you have first secured your own.

Rarely having attended rock concerts over the years I can likely list each one I have ever been to, starting with the Blackpool Opera House in 1984 (not sure that qualifies as a rock concert however). My nephew Alex also went to his first grown up concert at the Blackpool Opera House, in 2010, to see a band I had never heard of. I shared with him that this had been the scene of my first concert experience and Alex was reasonably impressed until I told him it was to see Wham! You had to be there Al. Following George Michael, I have seen (in no particular order) The Beautiful South (Sheffield), Simple Minds (Edinburgh), Martin Stephenson and the Daintees (Edinburgh and London), Pearl Jam (Toronto), Matchbox Twenty (Toronto), The Eagles (Toronto), David Gray (Toronto and Hamilton), Blue Rodeo (Oakville), Cold Play (Toronto) and Moxy Fruvous one Canada Day at Harbour Front in Toronto in the late nineties. The importance of mentioning Moxy Fruvous will become clear in a moment, not that I didn't enjoy the concert you understand.

In spite of this pitifully small, but select musical history, my concert regrets are few other than never having seen Queen live. I am not one to seek out crowds and I was never keen on queuing, standing, and not being able to hear my companions speak. Rock concerts are not designed for people like me. I am not, however, a cultural philistine as I passionately love the theatre, enjoy most ballet and *some* opera. Before I sound impossibly priggish I also love

Law & Order, Modern Family, crime fiction novels and the movies. Furthermore, I am fully aware which interests consume more of my free time hour for hour.

In May 2010 Lovely Husband and I managed to score some last minute well-priced tickets to see David Gray the following evening in Hamilton. We had seen Sir David on two previous occasions in Toronto, once at the Air Canada Centre where he was nothing shy of genius, and the second time at Massey Hall where everyone including DG seemed to be in a gloomy mood. Me because we (I) had a restricted view and Lovely Husband because he had bought the tickets months in advance for the price of a small car and the people around us had purchased their tickets earlier that day and claimed loudly to still have change left from $20. I cannot speak for DG. So after hearing DG interviewed on CBC Radio "Q" by the wonderful Jian Ghomeshi (thanks to a phone call from friend Luke to let me know JG was interviewing DG) we bought the tickets and went. A Saturday night in Hamilton is not a social practice with which I am familiar but hey David Gray is David Gray. Royal Wood was opening for DG and had brought with him World Vision who had set up booths in the lobby, how could you not love the guy? After RW and before DG I whispered to Lovely Husband that I was convinced Jian was in the building. Sir David was splendid and when the house lights came up after the final promise to "Meet Me on the Other Side" I spotted Jian getting up out of his seat a mere two rows in front. Immediately I clutched Lovely Husband's arm and remained fixed to the spot, fully aware that I had only that morning had my hair done, such luck. Lovely Husband, because he really is that Lovely, encouraged me to go and introduce myself and say hello because if I didn't, as he correctly pointed out, I would indeed regret it. Quick flick of the hair and over I go, blatantly, and probably somewhat rudely, interrupting the engaging Jian who at the time was in mid conversation. Jian was perfectly charming and offered a handshake as I approached, looking me in the eye perhaps a bit worried that he thinks he should know who I am but can't quite place, or maybe he feared he was about to be accosted by a stalker . . . . I then begin to stutter and gush. "Big fan, love the show, love David Gray, love you, love Q, love everyone." I could see the guy next to Jian rolling his eyes and I didn't care. I had let go, and I was looking up.

CHAPTER 6

STICK A PIN IN THE MAP AND DISCOVER THAT YOU LIVE HERE

"We make a living by what we get, but we make a life by what we give."

Winston Churchill

When Lovely Husband and I agreed to get married, which incidentally was not a foregone conclusion as we had both been married before and there was much to consider, we were eager to share the news with our nearest and dearest. With the date selected, June 14, we called our respective families one Sunday afternoon. My nephew Alex, who was 13 at the time, proclaimed to his older sister "from June, Ricardo is going to be our Uncle."

We laughed; pleased that the children were pleased and also highly amused that although Alex and Hannah certainly considered Lovely Husband to already be a part of the family, and part of their lives, for Al the defining act would take place "from June" thus cementing Lovely Husband's appointment to that of official relative.

Embracing a new role and adopting the title to accompany the position typically occurs with thoughtful deliberation, and often as not with a signature. You make a decision to become something and suddenly, officially, legally you are it.

Fifteen minutes in front of a Justice of the Peace, a couple of witnesses, a license, and a signing on the dotted line transforms you into a spouse. A resume submission, three rounds of interviews and a smile-less corporate photo proving you are in possession of the code to the photocopier, can turn you into a new hire. Studying for and passing a history test, filling in several forms and swearing your allegiance can turn you into the citizen of your country of choice, regardless of where you were born. There are endless positions for us to occupy and essentially in taking up the pen you can become whomever you choose, even down to legally changing your name.

I have thought about changing my name once or twice as an idle daydream and not, before you ask, upon the act of marriage. On occasion I have toyed with the idea of adopting a less cumbersome alias thereby avoiding the requirement to slowly enunciate each letter carefully to the listener in the manner of some overachieving Grade 5 Spelling Bee contestant every time I introduce myself. Usually I flirt with the idea of being a Catherine, Sarah, Virginia, or Alex (which admittedly would be somewhat confusing now with my nephew and all). I then attach this newly minted first name to a strong glamorous surname for road testing. For example Catherine Hampton, Sarah Walker, Virginia Van Mayer, Alex Barker, Sarah Walker-Barker, ah, the possibilities are endless. Lately I have been inclined to think of myself increasingly as a Veronica. On the way to Washington (see Chapter 9) I pronounced to Lovely Husband that my new handle was to be Veronica Buckle-Up. It was a long drive and I was reduced to focusing on the road signage throughout Pennsylvania to relieve the boredom of being a passenger who suffers from motion sickness and can barely send a text from the car without turning green. Incidentally in addition to being advised to fasten our seats belts other signs discouraged we drivers from picking up hitchhikers due to the proximity of the large state penitentiary. I must say Veronica Hitchhiker did not possess the same ring.

At my absolutely lovely friend Meg's 1970s themed birthday party a couple of years ago I donned a large curly wig, enormous sunglasses and black cocktail dress to become Ruby Babur a fictitious lead singer for the equally fictitious band *"Ruby and the Turtlenecks."* All this because Lovely Husband and our two splendid friends, Carla and Andre, from Montreal would only agree to wear a costume providing it involved nothing more complicated than black trousers and a black turtleneck sweater.

Take a moment and list your official positions. I suspect you will hit approximately twenty before you are required to devote any serious thought to the exercise. These are mine: spouse, daughter, sister, aunt, dog owner, friend, sister-in-law, cousin, business partner, business woman, entrepreneur, citizen (dual), coach, club member, political party member, board member, mentor, vendor, volunteer, trainer, facilitator, feminist, front-woman for fake band and yoga devotee. You could go on and on, tax payer, Honda driver, homeowner, customer, reader, writer, painter, horse rider, scuba diver, hat wearer, traveller, tweeter, cook, book club organizer, theater-goer, critic, reformed smoker, Niagara resident, obsessive compulsive towel-straightener . . . really, this could be anyone! Some of these carry weighty responsibilities, others are private and of little consequence to the world at large. What matters is not the title of the position of course but the effort one ploughs into living this position, and more importantly becoming the person behind the title and therefore worthy of the moniker.

I have been a cousin for years, since birth actually, but up until quite recently not a very good one. In fact I was a cousin in name only. I didn't do anything that made me a cousin. The same could be said for all positions, particularly those of privilege. Sure, you can make some vows, wear a big rock and a bigger frock, but what differentiates a de facto wife from a spouse emerges over time. The distinction is as they say between a wedding and a marriage. A wedding is an event, an expense of bubbles, whirlwind attention, canapés and cake. A marriage is a journey, marked along the route with communication, discussion, support, friendship and love, and reminders to "buckle-up Veronica." What makes you an Uncle is not the "from June" it is the effort, attention and affection you put into remaining connected and involved in the lives of your younger family members even at a geographic and generational distance. And as I have learned, whatever you bring to them, they bring back to you with abundance. All it takes is a conscious effort.

From the Lake Blog January 12, 2011: Muscle Memory

> *So far this week I have taken two pretty strenuous yoga classes, and after almost 3 weeks away from the mat my muscles are screaming and I am definitely out of practice. The amazing part to me is that although I took 159 yoga classes in 2010, and I am being specific here and not using my usual hyperbole, it took only 21 days away from the class to slide back down to a lesser level of expertise. Does this happen with our managerial, leadership, communication and coaching skills? If we don't use those muscles do we lose them? This morning during my practice I felt clumsy, awkward and heavy on my feet. The cowardly option is to simply walk away and not practice. I can easily convince myself I am far too busy after all and there really is a huge amount of snow on the ground etc. Is this what happens to us with our teams in providing constructive feedback or in managing poor performance? Have we simply neglected it for a couple of weeks and now cannot face starting up again? Well*

here is a tip for all of us: roll out your managerial mat and get back in the game, today. Your team needs you, whether you feel like it or not.

Self-help, meditation and yoga advice abound with the notion of *being present*. As we all know "the mind is a monkey" and unless we take charge we will fight the beast on an ongoing basis and be perpetually knocked off course. We suffer sleepless nights, poor concentration, diminished focus, and reduced decision making capability due to our inability to manage the mind. My friend Simon suggests the prevalence of poor attention spans during conversation, which is of course the moment at which we reveal this flaw to others, is similar to the behaviour displayed by our dogs when they are running around outside, stop suddenly in their tracks becoming immediately distracted. The pups are intently focused on one scent for several minutes and then, oh, quick, there goes a squirrel and their attention goes with it. In fact when Lovely Husband and I catch each other straying off topic we yell "squirrel." You would be surprised how often this happens. If we played "squirrel" as a drinking game we would all be pissed in 10 minutes.

"The mind is everything, what you think you become."

Buddha

I mentioned earlier that for the first four years spent living in Niagara I would have been willing and ready to relocate back to Toronto as soon as Lovely Husband gave the nod. I am not sure that is necessarily wholly accurate anymore and the reason is not that I love Toronto any less. The fact is I have learned to live in Niagara. I have opened my eyes and my heart to Niagara. I no longer describe where I live in terms of it being only so far from Toronto or in terms of rating the natural beauty, although without question this is a gorgeous place. "I presently live in Niagara" is no longer a statement alluding to my temporary residential state of mind. Present in Niagara is now a definitive statement of fact. I presently live in Niagara means I am sincerely present. I moved here in 2006 and now, five years on, I actually live here.

Living in Niagara, or anywhere for that matter, demands involvement. You could live in the number one Conde Nast Traveller city in the world and not love it or live in it fully. Whether you have occupied more than one page in your friends' address books or not, living where you live calls for a conscious commitment.

I am amused by the local councilors with their election leaflets summarizing the qualifications and skill that define and confirm their suitability for election to local office. Such bios usually begin with "as a lifelong resident of Wellsville Ontario." Curious that the idea of having lived somewhere for one's entire life becomes translated as "I remember when that condo building was all fields and am therefore the wise choice for your ward, vote for me." Again, perhaps not the most reliable and valid selection criteria, however aside from the unimaginative and underwhelming bios I give the candidates full credit for the grim and likely often thankless work they will have to perform upon successful election. They are at the very least making a conscious commitment to live where they live.

The natural beauty of this area initially overshadowed some of the startling realities surrounding my adopted town. We have Niagara Falls, one of the Natural Wonders of the World a mere twenty minute drive from our front door. We enjoy the orchards, vineyards, and endless access to the endless water, the escarpment, and the idyllic picturesque chocolate-box village that is Niagara-on-the-Lake. Even our own somewhat ordinary looking house from the front, harbours a delicious back garden secret in the form of yachts, boats, and ships passing soundlessly by 24 hours a day from April to January. Okay, now I am wondering why Niagara Falls, the Welland Canal and the Great Lakes have all failed to achieve UNESCO World Heritage status. I mean Bruges is on the list, and I have spent two nights in Bruges which although charming was in my opinion one night too many. Lovely Husband does on occasion still rave about the custard tarts he ate for breakfast in Bruges. And by the way, if you have not seen the movie *"In Bruges"* with Colin Farrell, Brendan Gleeson and Ralph Fiennes, you must.

According to the Social Assistance Reform Network of Niagara (SARNN), this is a "community in crisis" (Draper, 2010) and that between 2005-2009 Niagara lost 7000 manufacturing jobs (ibid). Draper's column for Niagara At Large, highlighting the SARNN work, goes on to say that some towns in the area report that over 70% of the population are living below the poverty line and for the past two years the Niagara regions' unemployment figures were among the highest in Canada. It is reported that in 2009 when a new hardware store held a job fair, prior to opening its doors, there were over 70 applicants per vacancy (Draper, 2010). Worryingly, the support for community-based programs is eroding in spite of the hefty efforts of legions of volunteers and front-line agencies, or maybe because of it. For example, Draper's article on the work of SARNN goes on to explain that in 2009 the YWCA Niagara lost the funding for its unique women's employment program. Cancelled. Gone. Unfunded. Popular thinking abounds with recognition that improving and securing employment prospects and economic independence for women are essential in tackling poverty.

> *"If you're looking for a cure for poverty in the world, the answer is to empower women."*
>
> Christopher Hitchens
> Munk Debates, November 26, 2010, Toronto

From the Lake Blog October 15, 2010: The 8 List

Canada's Top 100 Employers 2011 (published today) highlights a distinguished group of organizations. Congratulations to all those on the list and to all those who aspire to be on that list in the future. Below is the evaluation criteria:

1. *Physical Workplace*
2. *Work Atmosphere and Social*
3. *Health, Financial, Family Benefits*
4. *Vacations and Time Off*
5. *Employee Communications*
6. *Performance Management*
7. *Training and Skills Development*
8. *Community Involvement*

Take this opportunity to assess your own performance within each of these 8 areas. While we won't all make the list for 2012, (there are only 100 spots) consider what improvements in those 8 areas could do for your reputation as an employer, your relationships with you staff and customers, overall performance and ultimately your bottom line.

My Mother introduced me to public service, through example, and for as long as I can remember she has been an active member of her community. When My Sister and I were small we would accompany Mother as she delivered envelopes in our neighborhood, returning a week later to collect the same envelopes now filled with change to be counted and sent to those in need. We tagged along as Mother collected old clothes and jumble for the local Charity Shop, and would then work with Mother and others on the days when the Charity Shop was open. We would price items, help organize the shelves and no doubt generally be underfoot. On Saturday afternoons once or twice a month the three of us would head off to Garstang and the Cheshire Home where Mother would be *doing the teas*. The Cheshire Home was a large house set in beautiful grounds where My Sister and I would play for hours in the wooded areas going inside only when it rained, or when it was time to help serve the sandwiches, secretly hoping that we might end up with a bit of cake.

The Cheshire Home was essentially a long-term care facility for people of all ages with incurable diseases or conditions, and still, as far as I know, continues to provide this incredible service today. I remember vividly a young woman who had been involved in a climbing accident and was now spending the rest of her life in bed. I hated the hospital smell and likely as not complained about this to my then young Mum who briskly, devotedly and without comment went about her work with the efficiency and commitment of a woman who was a trained nurse.

In June 2008 my Mother attended a *hats will be worn* garden party at Buckingham Palace in recognition of her years of public service. Hilariously when the invitation to the event first arrived in the mail Mother's heart sank at the sight of the official looking envelope. Mother, incorrectly it turns out, assumed it was yet another speeding ticket having been caught on camera only a few weeks earlier.

Having been tutored at the knee of Ann Biswas I have volunteered my time and performed various acts of public service in the past and enjoyed doing so. I was a Samaritan in the UK and again, briefly, in Canada staffing phone lines on overnight duty. In Toronto I sat on a non-profit board for a highly impressive and well-run organization focused upon tackling homelessness, which sadly to this day remains a staggeringly significant problem in Canada's largest city. The focus for this non-profit was two-fold. Firstly to provide temporary housing solutions, and secondly to provide skill development for the clients who were dealing with crippling challenges while trying to get back in the game. It was well run largely due to the expertise and competence of the paid staff led by the Executive Director who was a superwoman and whom I still want to be when I grow up. I have to admit that I was and still am struck by the homelessness problems in cities around the world. Fourteen years later and not much has improved in Toronto regardless of who occupies the seat in Queen's Park.

When we lived in the Beach, Lovely Husband and I attempted to volunteer our time at a Toronto animal care organization. We sat through a mind numbing power point presentation one night after work with an assortment of like-minded willing Toronto citizens, and a few who were there as a punishment to complete their required levels of community service. After repeated chastisements from the rather frightening leader at the orientation session who firmly insisted, "everyone, and I mean *everyone* cleans cages" we quietly made a donation and slipped out of a side door.

In 2009 I volunteered to teach literacy skills to children with learning difficulties. I am not a gifted communicator when it comes to children, and they and I found the whole experience to be rather a strain. Each Sunday afternoon, prior to the Monday evening class, I would prepare my lesson plans with the gusto (or was that with the fear) of a junior supply teacher who had just received *the call*. There was no specific curriculum to follow, and in the absence of such a guideline the leaders directed us to websites that provided a glut of teaching resources mostly in the form of games. I am not terribly good at games, which may explain why I am not terribly good with children. One particular Monday evening after a weekend consumed with classroom prep, I pulled out my toolkit of coloured papers, stickers, pens and word based BINGO, with every expectation of wowing and impressing my young scholar. My usually eager student slumped his shoulders, barely concealed his disappointment and whispered under his breath "bingo, again." I was crushed.

In June 2010 I signed up to become a Board Member for a non-profit agency in Niagara whose mandate was to provide basic employment skills and training to those hoping to re-enter the job market following a significant absence. By September I was Chair of the Board, not because I bullied my way there or outshone my fellow board members but because I threw myself into it, fully and completely. The work mattered to me, the cause mattered to me. Sadly, in spite of the efforts and hard work from all involved that agency closed its doors a year later due to a lack of funding. I continue to be shocked and horrified at the plight of some residents in this community. Who knew this area had a drug problem, that in all probability is connected to, and in part responsible for, the ever-increasing prostitution problem. Some of the young people in the region are facing serious challenges, dropping through enormous education and social cracks, being identified as at risk in Grade 8 and in all honesty having the slimmest chances of finishing high school, and if that works out the way we all fear then very little chance of getting a job, anywhere. A fate such as this burdens the younger generations with a worse economic future than any of us could have imagined possible for a developed country in the twenty-first century.

I must stress the parallels I have drawn, highlighting the realities, shortcomings and travesties in this city, are far from exclusive to the Niagara Region. I am not holding up Southern Ontario to the harsh political sunlight as a delinquent example of municipal and provincial deficiency. My revelation is of a more personal nature and my motivation for doing so entirely constructive in intention. Over the last few years I confess to having ignored, forgotten, and neglected to look closely at what was going on around me. I was remiss in my lack of attention to those in trouble or simply less fortunate, bar the monthly cheque to my sweet child in Northern India, which I might add, is performed via direct debit and requires zero effort on my part. I am not even required to lick a stamp. Having lived to date what many would consider a charmed life, my constant struggles for purpose and fulfillment had rendered me to be self-centred to the point of exclusion. So focused was I in recent years on looking inward that any world outside of my own simply did not exist. Shamefully it had not occurred to me to look. Sure I read the papers, watched the news and huffed and tutted with the rest of the on-line irrates but of course didn't actually register a substantive view. I am a fine (make that bold) arguer, and can through years of practice, argue a point on almost any topic taking any view just for the sport of it. Had you listened to me across the dinner table or from the comfort of a warmly lit living room you would have thought me socially passionate and politically aware. Hot air aware only I am afraid to say. Good at the chat, stellar at the affronted who-do-they-think-they-are posturing, exceptional at digging up items for discourse, but all of this was superficial and lacking in meaning. The depths of my social conscience was indeed "shallow as a birdbath" as my friend Simon would say. And he would be right. How could I have lived in this community for over four years and be surprised at the extent of the community issues? The same community issues I might add that can be found in any Canadian city, or in any city in the world for that matter.

Through my old school friend Victoria, who lives in the UK, and I have known since we were four, I met a flight attendant with British Airways who called everyone "heart." That's what I was missing…I was missing heart. I loved the seemingly effortless brilliance of the Heart & Stroke campaign slogan, winningly encouraging us to participate, improve and take care of our health and the health of those around us, by urging us to "Put our hearts into it." That is precisely what was needed here. I needed to put my heart into my own life.

From Lovely Husband's Lake Blog June 14, 2010: These Guys Get It

During the past three weeks I have travelled to Vancouver Island and Regina for work with Clients, in both cases flying with WestJet. I must say I was very impressed. Courteous, friendly and efficient staff who were actually interested in the individual traveller, and to add to that the flights were on time. On-line check-in, call-centre responses, flight and ground crews all demonstrated a consistency of customer care that has now made them my airline of choice. At the Regina airport last Friday, I could see into the back room at the WestJet counter and spotted an employee communication poster that immediately caught my eye. Having checked-in I asked if I could have a closer look at the poster. Within 30 seconds I was speaking with a supervisor who was more than willing to answer the flood of questions I had regarding the program. We had a great discussion on the purpose of the initiative and how a local associate, to whom I was then introduced, had created it. The program creator was a charming woman, and very proud in an endearing modest way, here was an excellent example of Associate Engagement. What all of this says to me is that WestJet gets it.

From the Food Diary

June 5—Away So No Weigh (ASNW)

- Smoked salmon omelette, latte
- Pate, 2 pieces of French bread
- 3 glasses of red wine
- Spaghetti Bolognese

June 6—ASNW

- 2 poached eggs, 3 sausages
- 1 pear, slice brie
- 1 tin chickpeas, onion
- 2 glasses of wine
- 1 cup frozen yoghurt
- 1 teaspoon peanut butter

June 7—138lbs

- 2 eggs, toms, carrots
- 2 x large sausages
- 2 glasses of wine
- 1 chicken breast, cauliflower, mushrooms, onion

June 8—136lbs—60 minutes yoga

- All Bran, muesli, blueberries, milk
- Carrots, toms, mushrooms
- 1 chicken breast, onions, peas, dahl
- 2 glasses of wine

June 9—136lbs

- All Bran, muesli, blueberries, milk
- 1 tin tuna, 4 x beetroot
- 1 pear, carrots, toms
- Mince curry
- 2 glasses of wine
- 1 teaspoon p-bar

CHAPTER 7
THE THREE PS

"Our deepest fear is not that we are inadequate. Our deepest fear
is that we are powerful beyond measure. It is our light, not our
darkness, that most frightens us. We ask ourselves, who am I to be
brilliant, gorgeous, talented, and fabulous?
Actually, who are you not to be?"

Marianne Williamson, Return to Love 1992

Today in yoga class we were practicing some rather strenuous moves packed full of threes. Three-legged dog, three-legged plank, and my all time leg-burning favourite warrior three, which we performed no less than, oh yes, three times, on each leg I might add, for what felt like three hours at a time. And you remember how I feel about odd numbers. After seemingly endless crows, eagles, cranes and other birds that I began to loath, Jane the instructor, directed us to put our palms flat on the mat ahead of us, bend one leg and place the sole of that foot on the mat and with the other leg in the air (are you still with me?) she then encouraged us to commence the small hops required to lift both legs in the air as if going into a good old fashioned schoolyard handstand. I can do a handstand, underwater. As soon as Jane mentioned "handstand" I groaned inwardly and my immediate thought was, "I can't do that, haven't done an on-land-handstand since I was 8 years old." Yet, because of Jane, because she is an excellent teacher in a stretch you to your limits kind of way, I gave it a go. And although I did not manage the full handstand I did enjoy those sacred moments where for just a few almost perfect seconds you are temporarily suspended in the air, not as the result of a hurried hop, but because you are breathing correctly and using your core.

At the start of the third quarter in 2010 in my first year of self-employment, I was feeling a pressing need to close the sale, seal the deal, and amass an armload of signed bullet proof contracts. Business development is an ongoing practice for the self-employed and one wonders constantly if each new gig will be the last. In the midst of the euphoria that comes with securing a new piece of work the back of your mind Nelly reminder is ever present, muttering, "Well, okay, you got one more, but this, this will be the end of it." Standing frozen with fear peering into the deep hole, wringing your hands and waiting for the well to dry up is neither a good look nor useful practice. Consulting is unique in that it is highly unlikely anyone will think to look for your services in the yellow pages, there is not the slightest chance a Client will wander into your virtual store, or respond to your ad on Craig's list even if you put it there in six feet high flashing neon.

In addition to the networking, advocated by many as at least a good start, Lake and Associates started to get creative. Lovely Husband had performed some pro bono work in the previous year, which, by the way, if anyone is looking to break into a new market is an excellent strategy. As the Consultant, working for free provides the opportunity to road test and refine your models, ideas and approaches. You can make a few adjustments along the way and receive candid feedback on your work from a person who has a vested interest in your success in that they want you to do well for them (as well as for you) and therefore encourages you to keep going. For their part, the Client receives guidance and expertise without incurring the expense. Assuming you do a good job, and why wouldn't you, the Client then sends referral business your way and in doing so becomes a champion for you, which truly is a gift when you are out there on your own.

During our new idea generation moments, and we had several necessity being the mother of invention and all that, we opened our minds, our outlook broadened and we embraced the unknown. In concert with this harmonization of creative forces we disagreed, argued and at times threw our toys out of the pram, which I firmly believe is perfectly acceptable and all part of the process.

Up until the middle of 2010 I had remained a social media neophyte. Later in the summer my nephew Alex attempted to sell me on the features and benefits of Facebook. I replied that Facebook really wasn't for me. Alex looked at me with complete sincerity and shaking his head said wisely, "Auntie Rash, Facebook is for everyone." One Lake and Associates advisor, Henry, who possesses extensive expertise in marketing, strongly encouraged us to revamp our website and start blogging and tweeting. Good grief, blogging and tweeting sounds like a rather embarrassing medical condition. "Ah God love her, she was blogging and tweeting right to the end." I confess I had considered both of these activities to be self-centered nonsense for those low on friends, lacking in social skills, and overly blessed with free time, and I could not see how a business such as ours might benefit. Sure I was on LinkedIn because that was for professionals.

I mention Henry, one of our advisors, as throughout the evolution of Lake we learned the value of seeking input from those who firstly understood our business and secondly cared about us sufficiently to offer candid advice and feedback. Better yet are those who offer guidance accompanied with constructive suggestions, having taken the time to thoughtfully consider their responses, and in true "*Lovecat*" style (Tim Sanders) offer to and then do connect you with others. These are the folks who genuinely have your best interests at heart. We owe sincere thanks to Diane, Clive, Luke, Jim, Henry, and several others all for different reasons and they all know why.

We invested the money and re-worked the website. The transformation was phenomenal. Not only were we proud to show it off for its good looks, we were also blown away by its new found functionality whereby the technology had actually begun to partner with the business. In some cases it was as simple as being able to utilize PayPal to process payments for participants in upcoming workshops. In later iterations it gave us a platform from which to showcase the stories of established and start-up women entrepreneurs, an area of specific interest to me in particular. These stories documented in the L.I.F.E. series (Lake Interviews Female Entrepreneurs) succeed in driving much increased traffic to the site, and helped us further differentiate Lake and Associates in a crowded and growing consulting arena. We morphed into identifying ourselves as the entrepreneur's choice when it came to consulting. We blogged. We wrote. They came. They read. Admittedly at first our primary audiences were immediate family members but gradually we discovered we had a loyal following of readers. One unfortunate by-product of tweeting is that I am now obsessively checking my followers and feel offended and wounded when I inevitably lose someone as they decide to move on and "unfollow" me. It reminds me of being kicked off a sports team or being overlooked for a party invitation. I am not sure why the company of strangers on-line matters to me but I cannot pretend to be unaffected even in some minor way. As I write my BlackBerry is flashing with the news that I have picked up a new follower . . . is someone watching? And what clever musings, announcements and all round witticisms must I create in order to keep my new fan engaged?

Self-promotion is a wile creature. I suspect many of us who were raised in the 60s and 70s by thoroughly middle class parents were taught to hold back, refrain from boasting and allow others to go first. Shining our own lights in midlife can be unfamiliar territory and yet a requirement nonetheless.

From the Lake Blog August 23, 2010: Are You Getting What You Deserve?

My niece Hannah is having a great week. Last Thursday she, along with all the other A-level students in the UK, received her exam results. Hannah got the grades she needed and has secured her place at the University of her choice and for the course of her choice. Hannah is a bright girl and she worked hard. My Sister and I observed that Hannah did in fact get what she deserved. To top off her week Hannah passed her driving test, but back to the exam results. When I was 18 and heading for university, the headmaster at my school, Arnold School in Blackpool, spoke at the Leavers' Assembly and stated simply but dryly that he hoped we would all get what we deserved. Clearly this has stuck with me. Are you getting what you deserve from your business or from your work? Is it time for a back-to-school tune up and to assess whether you need to change your effort, your focus, your input, style, approach or attitude in order to ensure you positively get what you deserve in the coming months?

During my corporate years I held on to a misplaced belief that if I performed great work and continued to work harder I would be promoted. I was wrong. I learned, albeit rather too late for that particular world and that particular time, that one not only had to work hard and perform outstanding work, one had to talk about it. One had to describe one's achievements and take ownership for them. I have never had a problem admitting my mistakes however I graduated from the collaborative school of leadership where mangers included others at every turn when it came to reaping the rewards of praise for a job well done. "Team effort" was a phrase with which my lips were familiar.

Beware what you say to others whether good or bad, positive or negative, self-deprecating or brash. In my experience whichever angle you choose for your personal and professional spin you will be believed providing you remain just this side of credible. Look at politicians who are elected primarily on the basis of what they say, and what they say they intend to do. You can argue re-election is dependent upon actions but bear with me here. Tell someone "I love you" and they will in all probability believe you, even if your actions prove otherwise. It can take a long time to recognize the incongruity between the spoken word and the action. And they say actions speak louder than words yet I am not so sure as I think we hear what is convenient and reconstruct the actions in order to make sense of it all. This is not because we are necessarily naïve, no, simply put it is typically because we are all so busy with our own lives that we rarely take the trouble to dig deeply into the life of another in the bold quest of searching for the truth. It is in all honesty too much like work, and frankly who has the time?

From the Lake Blog November 20, 2010: Silence is Not Golden For High Performers

Coaching and feedback is sometimes reserved for discipline and corrections. All too often high performance renders silence from a manager, coach or leader. Whether an employee is performing well or under performing, they need to hear about it and they need to hear about it from their immediate manager. Busy managers, which includes just about everyone, often describe lack of time as the main reason for failing to coach in general, and certainly for failing to coach the superstars. The short response is to make time. By recognizing good performance and by asking your best employees what is contributing to their success you will likely increase motivation and no doubt learn something you can share. Recognize, ask, and share.

With that in mind if you tell me you run 12 miles each evening when you return home from your 10 hour day followed by 90 minute commute, are learning Cantonese in your spare time while raising triplets and working on your MBA, I will likely as not, choose to believe you. So if I rather foolishly was falsely modest when being congratulated for my efforts I have no one to blame but myself, and see, now you believe me.

That isn't to say the Billy Liars among us won't be hunted down and exposed without the pack even breaking a sweat. If your stories are too tall you will be branded as such. A friend of mine attended a rather fancy dinner party some time back and retells the tale of being seated next to a boorish chap who spoke endlessly of his accomplishments which, if the listener did so carefully, made the fool sound more accomplished than Steve Jobs, Gandhi and Hillary Clinton put together. One can take it a tad too far.

With a combination of admiration and occasional bewilderment, I applaud those for whom no audience is too small, and consider no situation inappropriate when it comes to loudly and publicly extolling their own virtues. In practice when it comes to friendship I lean firmly towards those with at least a smattering of humility. I remember fondly an executive I worked with who at a particularly nauseating mine-is-bigger-than-yours meeting was the most senior guy in the room and put an end to all the titles and posturing that was going on even at the introduction stage by stating simply "my name is Peter and I'm from marketing." Peter shut everyone up and I loved him on sight.

Knowing when to brag and when to blush are skills indeed. No one wants to become the idiot who claims to have secretly advised the Queen while simultaneously fighting for human rights in Somalia (unless of course it is true) however there are times when it is required that we step up and shine. Furthermore, having a sense of how and when to showcase one's talent is a fine balance between assertiveness and restraint. There maybe several successes you would like to shout from the rooftops however not everyone wants or needs to hear them. The key is to be selective, know your audience and practice the art of timing because ultimately, in spite of those for whom schadenfreude is a recreational sport, we all love a success story and you are obliged to share.

If you follow the business magazines, books, newspapers, and on-line sources, there are endless stories charting the rise of various executives, leaders and entrepreneurs. I am hooked on these stories and particularly enjoy the LA Times column *"How I Made It"* although I confess I always read *Health: Fitness and Nutrition* first which inspires me to reach for the oatmeal or get myself out the door and head to yoga. On the business front I love hearing about the career paths taken by others and am always fascinated to read how this person started their professional life as a marine biologist and is now a great success in the fashion industry.

Arguably there can be no greater "making it in business" success story in Canada than that of Frank O'Dea. As a young man in his early twenties Frank O'Dea had taken some tough turns, found himself homeless and on occasion slept on the streets of Toronto. For those not familiar with his story, O'Dea went on to co-found Second Cup in 1975. Today Second Cup is the largest gourmet coffee and tea franchise retailer in the country with 340 outlets across Canada, and in my opinion they serve the best blueberry muffins.

I delight in the idea of a young Ralph Lauren starting out by selling his creatively designed ties to Bloomingdales in the late sixties and going on to develop the incredible Ralph Lauren empire. I imagine the first Zara store, founded by Armancio Ortega, opening its doors in Galicia, Spain, and now they open their doors each morning in over 70 countries.

Driving to Burlington for a meeting the other morning, I listened to a radio interview with the legendary Joan Rivers. I remember my friend Victoria and I recording a stand-up routine of Joan's onto VHS tape from the telly when we were about eighteen. Joan was rude, funny and self-deprecating. Victoria and I watched her over and over, quoting the punch lines with Joan until I am sure the tape eventually broke or one of our Mother's threw it out for fear we would fail our exams if we didn't switch it off and finish our A-level law revision. I loved and still love Joan Rivers' voice as much as anything else about her. Ms. Rivers seemed so bold to us at that time, and indeed she was and still is. We were living fairly cosseted lives in a small town in the north of England where our world and our routines revolved around school, friends, food, surreptitious smoking and drinking, hockey, learning to drive, studying for A-levels and boys. Joan Rivers was unlike any woman I had ever met or even heard. I was shocked, appalled and deeply impressed. The more recent radio interview focused its attention upon the launch of the Joan Rivers 2010 documentary "A Piece of Work" which I have not yet seen but is on my list and would have watched the other night had Cogeco not rudely interrupted the Pay Per View broadcast I had ordered due to error 8746. During the radio interview, on the phone from LA, Joan was poignant and candid discussing the realities of finding herself in recent years "playing clubs in the Bronx at 4:30pm on a Tuesday." I get the fact that Joan with her outspoken approach may not have made many friends in her business although it never seems to affect a man in the same way, clichéd but true. Turn on the tube and legions of chaps saying nasty things about anyone they choose and being considered kings of late night funny in the process will inundate you. The point of my mentioning the spectacular Joan Rivers is that she is the ultimate survivor and business success story, who, in spite of shattering setbacks, at the age of 70 something is not afraid to reinvent herself and does so with full and earnest capability. Ms. Rivers is driven by a seemingly insatiable desire to work and achieve and best of all Joan appears to ignore her critics, or maybe she does listen and then chooses to put the criticisms where they belong.

Starting your own business can be a clear case of "hurry up and wait." Patience and I have never been close friends and that had to change if I was to survive the torment of waiting that inevitably comes with the self-employment territory. There is much waiting in entrepreneurship in my experience, which is ironic given that one spends so much time running flat-out to launch the business and get it moving. Patience and perpetual motion are strange bedfellows.

As a vendor and service provider one can be low on the list of Client priorities in spite of Clients calling you for help. It is only to be expected that everyday work can get in the way of planning, training, team development or leadership coaching for many businesses. For some our services are a nice to have, for others we are essential. Knowing which is which teaches a good lesson for Client and Consultant alike. Consequently one waits for meetings, often to have them rescheduled, one waits for responses to proposals and one waits for the project start date. This is in no way a complaint, it is a fact, and the sooner I caught on to that, well, simply the better it was for all concerned.

We learned some important lessons during this process and I will share with you the Top 3 *Lessons from Lake* when it comes to closing the sale based on our experience of the first six months in business:

Patience: Firstly, never rule out a meeting, encounter or connection as a dead end until this had been categorically proven to be true, and only then because you absolutely unequivocally do not have what the Client is looking for, such as the ability to deliver technical equipment training, underwater, in Greek.

We have several excellent examples which support the claim that one must "never say never" as they say. For example, July 2010 we meet with a connection in the hope of providing some seminar work to augment an existing program. The conversation went well, we enjoyed meeting each other and agreed to remain in contact clear on the understanding when we parted that there was no immediate work on the horizon. November 2010 I send a follow up to this contact with a hey-how-are-you email and receive a nice note back, although still aware there was no work in sight. Months later an email arrives from the same connection asking if we are interested in providing seminar work in the fall. A couple of notes back and forth and we agree to run a two day workshop in November 2011. Sixteen months from start to finish. This is patience.

In-Person: The second *Lesson from Lake* in closing the sale is to only deliver proposals to Clients in person, unless you have to book an airline ticket to achieve this. So, assuming you and your Client are in the same time zone, get in your car and drive to meet the client at their convenience to deliver and review the proposal. You will no doubt encounter occasional resistance from Clients who are of course simply so busy that they would prefer to receive the proposal via email. Do not be put off. The project is important to the Client otherwise they would not have called.

You must deliver the content of the proposal in person so that you can:

a. Provide context and show your understanding of the business problem

b. Establish the link between the problem and your proposed solution

c. Demonstrate the value you and your firm bring to the project, your "You Resources."

d. Further develop a relationship with the Client

e. Answer questions

f. Ask questions

g. Secure next steps

In the early days, I would spend hours and hours developing proposals, agonizing over each word and sentence, shifting language to a minute degree, focusing upon nuance, and ensuring I captured every essence of the issue. Clients are business people with packed agendas so when receiving a proposal via email with the promise from me to meet and discuss later that day or the next (which I incorrectly thought would be helpful to the Client) no one read the damn thing, properly, or otherwise. I was naïve to think they would. No, instead you show up, put a big smile on your face and give the Client a copy after you have taken them through a spoken discussion / presentation (without a deck) that demonstrates your knowledge of the issue and your ability to deliver a solution. Live and in person is the only way to go.

I regret to admit we learned the second lesson the hard way, and eventually, after finally clueing in, our close rates improved dramatically. Although of the 3 leaders Ana and I never managed to beat Lovely Husband, who with a 100 percent close rate, was the Lake and Associates Employee of the Year in 2010 complete with requisite named parking space at Ana's house.

Persistence: The third *Lesson from Lake* on the matter of closing is to follow up, follow up follow up. We learned this from various advisors and also from direct experience. Just because the Client goes quiet does not mean you do. It is definitely not over until it is over and only then because the Client has taken out a restraining order against you.

Patience, In-Person and **Persistence** are the three Ps of closing the sale . . . . in our experience.

Naturally if the project lead time is over a year, which realistically can be the case, you must have multiple irons in the fire which takes us full circle back to the business development activities. Feeding the mouth of the sales cycle is a constant feature of your daily life as an entrepreneur. I would sometimes watch the seemingly non-existent progress of building projects, or in particular road improvement and construction jobs, as I drove across the 400s all over Ontario and it would occur to me that you could in all likelihood show up everyday, and for a fairly long time, not do too much work and probably get away with it as there is nothing much to see for the effort on a daily basis. It's a bit like dieting or building an Olympic village. However, sooner or later someone asks the question and after six months or so there bloody well ought to be something to show for the endeavour. You may not look as if you are losing weight on a daily basis but at some point the day of *that event* will arrive and *that dress* is waiting for your body and you should be able to comfortably climb inside after all your hard work. At some point the athletes will arrive and be looking for a track to run on and a bed to sleep in.

We must pile on the effort to make it happen and if we don't we will be caught out in the end. Almost all activities worth the outcome take time, energy and an ongoing commitment. Saving money, paying off a mortgage, raising well adjusted children, studying for your degree, building good relationships, developing a strong reputation, achieving killer abs, whatever it is that matters to you all necessitate Patience, Persistence and likely as not, an In-Person appearance.

Footnote: *"Never Sold a Lipstick"* was the working title of a book I toyed with writing in the late nineties. *"Never Sold a Lipstick"* refers to a two-year project I pursued in an attempt to develop a line of cosmetics for women with darker complexions, who at that time (1997-99) were remarkably under catered to. I myself was always wearing the wrong colour, and have some frightful looking photographs to prove it. Having attended a cosmetics trade show in New York City I found a Toronto based cosmetics manufacturer who offered me great support. I loved going to their lab, talking colours and I recall how patient and willing they were with such an obvious novice, but they believed in the idea. I worked with a talented graphic designer who created a fabulous logo and brand identity. I named, trademarked and registered the company "WOW Cosmetics" (Women of the World) and generally put my heart, soul and hard earned cash into getting it off the ground. Holt Renfrew even invited me to a pitch meeting which actually went rather well considering I only had a basket of samples and the most basic of promotional ideas. I wrote the requisite business plan and sought venture capital and or angel financing. I was unsuccessful in obtaining the necessary funds to launch the line and tucked WOW back in the closet and got a day job. I think this fairly typical plight is technically referred to as being starved back to work. The key message here is that when starting out it is essential to secure alternate income streams as we have seen how long it can take to become an overnight sensation. If you are not funded it is mighty hard to stay focused. As Virginia Wolf commented, "If a woman is to write, she needs money and a room of her own."

From the Food Diary

<u>July 1—weight 138lbs—60 minutes yoga</u>

- All Bran, Meg's homemade granola, raspberries, milk
- 1 tin tuna, 2 teaspoons mayo, 4 x beetroot, 2 x Ryvita
- 10 carrots, 10 almonds
- 2 sausages, ½ tin baked beans
- 2 glasses of wine, 4 teaspoons Nutella

<u>July 2—weight 136lbs</u>

- Blueberry muffin
- Chilli, salad
- 20 almonds, 2 x olives
- 2 glasses of champagne, 2 glasses of wine

<u>July 3—weight 135lbs</u>

- Al Bran, blueberries, milk
- 1 x sausage, 30 almonds
- Salad, asparagus, 2 x sausages, 2 x chicken legs
- 1 glass bubbles, 2 glasses of wine

<u>July 4—Pretend to be American and Take a Holiday From The Scales</u>

- All Bran, blueberries, milk
- 1 cup 3 bean salad, half a chicken breast
- Oatmeal, blueberries, milk

- 2 glasses of wine
- Several teaspoons of Nutella

July 5—weight 135lbs—60 minutes yoga

- All Bran, Meg's homemade granola, blueberries, milk
- Mince curry
- ½ melon, yoghurt, 2 teaspoons Nutella

July 6—weight 136lbs—60 minutes yoga

- ¼ melon, All Bran, blueberries, Meg's homemade granola, milk
- Carrots, 12 almonds
- Mince curry
- 2 glasses of wine
- Yoghurt, 3 teaspoons Nutella

CHAPTER 8
SPEND IT WISELY

"Until you value yourself you will not value your time.
Until you value your time you will not do anything with it."

M. Scott Peck

A by-product of the changes I had made in 2010 was that I was able to spend more time with those who loved me and whom I loved back. That isn't to say I managed to see everyone who is important to me in 2010. Most notably I did not see my parents from September 2009 until December 2010 but at least I did eventually lay eyes on The Parents at the end of the year and give them a hug in time for my Father's 80th birthday, who being a good Hindu was born on Christmas Day (at least we think so, long story, poor record keeping in India in 1930 etc).

The summer in particular brought its own joy and happy times as Lovely Husband and I spent two glorious weeks in Portugal with My Sister and Clive, and assorted kids and friends who came and went throughout the fortnight. In addition to that we brought my niece Hannah to Canada for 10 days as her 18th birthday present from Lovely Husband and me.

I may have spent much of the year focusing-forward-with-cut-price-tuna, paying myself from savings more than once, no longer spending $100 each time I set foot in a Shoppers Drug Mart, and I dare say one or two spas, clothing and shoe stores were missing me terribly, but the time available to me was, as the ad says, priceless.

I had moved to Canada when my niece was four and my nephew had yet to wear out a pair of shoes. To say you miss out is an understatement. Of course, you have traded one set of experiences for another, and in all honesty I would not go back and change any of those decisions even if it were an option. Actually, when my parents were last here we had one of those conversations about when and where were you most happy and if you could revisit a time in your life when would that be. My response was firm in that I am happiest here and now and would not consider for a moment a time in the past that was preferable to the present. The most pressing argument being that if I lived it all again, only choosing different paths, I would not be married to Lovely Husband and would not know all the wonderful people that I am now so fortunate to have in my life. It has taken me years, and thousands of miles, to build this circle of friends and I could not imagine giving them up.

It was actually my good friend Carla who gave me the idea as to what to buy Hannah for her 18th birthday. The kid wants for nothing, thankfully, and Carla (a much loved Aunt herself) wisely advised that all your nieces and nephews really want from you is your time. So, our time is what she got. Ten, Hannah-centric days, spent in Ontario, smothered and spoiled to within an inch of her life by her Auntie Rash, Uncle Ricardo and cousin Molly. This was by no means Hannah's first visit to Canada but it was her first trip to visit us alone, a travel defining moment that I know she will remember. It is debatable as to who was more excited on the lead up to her visit, Hannah or us, and needless to say I planned almost every moment with the military precision (actually it was reminiscent of organizing corporate conferences) that you might expect from a doting Aunt with OCD tendencies.

Hannah's Visit

	Morning	Afternoon	Evening
Friday			7pm Hannah lands at the airport
Saturday	Out for breakfast Niagara-on-the-Lake	3pm Pedicures	Out for dinner DQ for ice cream
Sunday		Swim at Charlotte's	Family dinner at home
Monday	IHOP Niagara Falls	Maid of the Mist Be tourists	Watch *Love Actually* on DVD while lying on the sofa eating chips and chocolate
Tuesday	Bike ride along the Niagara river	Boat trip up the Niagara river	Dinner in NOTL Falls by night
Wednesday		Shaw Festival *The Women*	Drive-in movie *The Switch*
Thursday	St Jacob		
Friday	Horse riding along the Escarpment	Hannah bake banana bread	Dinner at Charlotte's Fort Erie Haunted Walk
Saturday	Drop Molly in Toronto	Luke & Simon's	Dinner at Julian's Overnight Luke & Simon's
Sunday	Cobourg		Watch 32 episodes of *Friends* on DVD while lying on the sofa eating like 9 year olds
Monday		Hannah to the airport for 6pm flight	House too quiet, me quiet cry

Children of my own never featured in my future and often over the years, and more frequently lately, this has become something of a conversation stopper. For example the exchange typically goes something like this:

Question: "Do you have children?"

Answer: "No."

Deafening silence.

At which point both I and the speaker feel obliged to fill the awkward silence that inevitably ensues, and continues to grow, lingering painfully as we individually search our minds frantically for a suitable follow up statement or comment. Sometimes I will offer up a hollow laugh, accompanied by a pseudo knowing smile and fill said silence with "Noooo, no, I have a dog" which can truly mystify some listeners, and actually mystifies me a little bit too, but I keep saying it. I am like a dogmatic comedian with a poor punch line who is convinced that if he can just find the *right* audience his joke will be declared funny after all, and, phew, he will be vindicated, or better yet, syndicated.

A childfree woman of a certain age is seen as a threat to a few and considered an anomaly to many. I have engaged in arguments with a variety of people in a range of settings over the years over my childless / childfree state. I had a particularly troubling exchange with a middle aged cab driver, with strong views on the matter, a few months back, who, having picked me up at 7am, and upon swiftly discovering my failure to breed, then spent the next 12 minutes interrogating and questioning me in order to unearth the root cause of my familial neglect. I suspect he was also attempting to convince me to see the error of my ways, run home to Lovely Husband immediately and spend the remainder of the day righting this apparent wrong. I consciously attempted to remain calm, successfully I might add, and relaxed my anger muscles as the taxi driver's protestations grew to a lively early morning crescendo of disbelief. I concentrated on smiling to myself, determined not to be ruffled or offended. Although I was absolutely offended and annoyed. I don't care if the taxi driver was well intentioned or not, it is no one's business but mine although apparently that is not always sufficient. I should know better than to engage in superficial pleasantries with single-minded bored and boorish strangers and I cannot for the life of me remember how this taxi driver turned interviewer managed to wrestle such highly personal information out of me. In my defence I am not much of a morning person. And what is it about the confines of a cab that make us think it is acceptable to probe into the private life of a total stranger and paying customer at that? I only remember saying "good morning, Queens Quay please."

The real interest here is not in delving into my psyche as to why I have never felt the maternal urge, no the mystery lies in why others find it so hard to comprehend. At times one feels as if one has broken some social rule or secret code of conduct. In not having children you have actually let the side down in your failure to give birth. Given the size of the world's population, exceeding 7 billion at last count, accusing me of jeopardizing the future of human kind is a pretty flimsy basis for criticism. It is as if you somehow didn't get the memo that we are all supposed to bear children, raise them in good circumstances or bad, and carry on regardless, happy or not. Just like at the Toronto animal care centre where everyone has to clean cages, and you Missy are no exception.

Many of the parents I see are fraught with anxiety when it comes to facing their relentless daily challenge of raising children. Money, time, patience and sleep all in short supply, always. I also know marvelously, almost effortless looking, natural parents who were born to guide and care for small people. My Sister immediately comes to mind, and from observation I consider her to be an incredibly skilled parent. And from their behaviour I know Hannah and Alex (who would after all be best placed to comment) feel the same. You should see the way they look at her.

To parent or not to parent must surely come down to choice. With the availability of birth control (in the West at least) deciding to have children or not is precisely that, a decision. Conceivably, pun intended, no other decision we make is so readily and presumptuously questioned by others. However, I hasten to clarify the decision in question is the one *not to have*. We do not seem to be questioned about deciding to have children unless we are deemed by broader society to be too young, too old, or already have too many in the minds of the all-knowing others. In particular I think of the, in my opinion, spectacularly judgmental *Daily Awful* tabloid newspapers, the middle England, middle class papers, casting disapproving eyes on mothers old and young alike.

Part of me thinks parents (Ps) are secretly envious of the non-parents (NPs), although many Ps claim to *feel sorry* for the NPs. Ps imagine NPs having more money, sex, time, energy, freedom, stress-free lives and argument-free households. It is certainly in line with what I think, although I wouldn't presume to judge you for your choice. Are the childfree like the political left who, it is argued, are too polite to call it as they see it (Westen, 2007) and therefore destined to remain on the social margins, forever behind on the tables of understanding and being understood? Are the NPs to be rendered social outcasts, incomplete as humans, and certainly not permitted to hold a single opinion on anything remotely connected to children? Seems to me that plenty of right-wing male politicians have much to say on the subject of birth control, and share their opinions freely with a view to imposing upon others their beliefs regarding the freedom of choice in particular and women's health in general. Read Drew Westen's fabulous book *The Political Brain* for his brilliant, and provocative explanation of his theory as to why the left lose when really they should win. Fascinating.

Regardless of our parenting status, our time is valuable and we must make conscious decisions as to how we spend it. Plenty of your time will be lost throughout the course of a normal day and as such we must be cautioned against simply misplacing the remainder. Think for a moment of all the hours that are silently taken from you? "*Stuck in Traffic*" an article in Maclean's magazine by the National Editor Andrew Coyne, cited the hours and days the average Canadian spends each year commuting. The figure is estimated to be the equivalent of an almost unbelievable 32 working days a year spent sitting in traffic (Coyne, 2011). This is your time being systematically robbed from under your nose.

What would you do with an additional 32 working days of free time? Imagine now that your entire year, to spend as you see fit, is actually only 11 months instead of the 12 you assumed (and who can blame you) that you thought were getting. Your three score and ten are now only three score and three. Think about it, living to eighty and in actuality living one full dog year less. Okay, you may not lose 32 days a year for 80 years but I suspect if we look hard enough we can find lost years throughout every cycle of life. Sleeping as a baby and as a teenager. Watching telly for hours. Arguing pointless arguments. Being angry, frustrated and upset. Complaining, now there is a good one. Sulking, dreaming up excuses, cancelling events, blaming others, being jealous, and ironing pillowcases. I have been known to iron pillowcases but am now resolutely sold on the fact that my house is not a Bed & Breakfast and creased but clean linens are acceptable.

Inevitably we cannot exercise absolute authority over every minute of our time but we can, likely as not, make significant improvements if we pay close attention and treat our time with the same reverence we would any other resource. *Killing time* has got to be the most ridiculous expression, and I long ago vowed to ban it from my own vernacular. You may not be able to eradicate the commute from your life, however you may be able to weigh up the pros and cons of why you are commuting. If the ends are worth it, then jolly good. If not, then it is time to think again and revaluate those decisions.

Furthermore, all this soppy nonsense about living today as if it were your last is in my view total bullshit. If today were my last day I sure as chips wouldn't have had oatmeal for breakfast or tuna and quinoa salad for lunch. Assuming I had it on pretty good authority that today was the end of the line for me then I would wake up to a huge bowl of the best vanilla ice cream I could find, no doubt full-fat-straight-on-the-hips strength. I very much doubt I would engage in anything remotely work related and instead would spend the day calling everyone I loved, and hopefully having talked to everyone by mid-afternoon, clear out my savings account and fly via private jet to New York City for dinner and spend my last night at the Ritz Carlton, Premier Park Suite of course, with Lovely Husband, never to wake up again in this life. I say NYC because although there are a thousand places I can think of to spend my last hours on earth, Paris, London, Mumbai, Buenos Aries, Sydney, My Sister's house surrounded by family, time is rather of the essence here so I don't want to waste half the day in the air as you might appreciate. Not intending to be morbid, merely practical.

Far from living each day as if it were your last, I propose living each day as if it was your first. In other words, live today as if you are going to live for a very long time. Not in the "oh I can do that tomorrow" sort of way, but instead with a sense of newness, curiosity, renewal, freshness, clear thinking, no baggage, self-discipline, and aspirations for accomplishment. Imagining you will live, and live well at that, for a very long time requires a specific shift in focus to secure a future based on longevity in all areas of your life while living firmly in the present, ensuring you plan for a good future, and not being concerned with or consumed by the past.

Living daily as if for a long life is the secret to getting the most out of every day. Living for a long life requires us to use the day creatively, putting our hearts into what and whom we love, giving back, building permanence, and applying our talents. Treat every day like your first day at a new job. Be a great big bloody keener. Living a long life demands we eat well, exercise, and generally look after ourselves. Saving money where it makes sense and where you can, spending money with thoughtfulness, and focusing upon building and maintaining meaningful relationships that you will come to rely on in the many years ahead. Living each day as if it was your first brings a lifetime and a daytime of possibilities without a single regret.

Living a full life, for me, demands a high level of organization, and I believe some of us are more equipped to deal with multi-tasking than others. I will avoid discussion of this nature along gender generalizations as I think that it is too easy and thoughtless an avenue to pursue. So allow me to offer a glimpse into my own experience. When focused on and consumed by climbing the slippery corporate slopes I did little else with my time. In my mind, and in my spirit, I did not feel I had room for anything more. At times I have been guilty of a supreme lack of imagination and pursued an extremely limited set of outside interests. I was singularly convinced it was all about the work, in spite of the fact that this tunnel vision focus was, ironically, not actually working out too well for me. Any extracurricular was mostly along the lines of going to the gym, drinking wine with my friends, shopping, and complaining about my job. Rarely would I do anything remotely worthwhile with my Sunday other than wait to go back to work on Monday. Staggeringly, I would spend almost the entire day in a state of uneasy apprehension and anticipation awaiting the morning alarm. I distinctly recall spending frequent weekday mornings making my bed and thinking to myself that I could not wait to return here that evening and climb in.

In the early days of Lake I would spend hours confined to my office and tethered to the desk, putting in the hours creating workshops and churning out product that never saw the light of day. This was entirely self-imposed and as my wise friend Toby pronounces is no doubt the result of years of conditioning. My rationale for performing this somewhat pointless and undoubtedly unproductive and essentially nothing-more-than-drudge work was the unshakeable belief that I must work eight hours a day at least five days a week in my new role as an entrepreneur. I had to put the time in. However, I was so busy putting the time in I neglected to ensure I was working on the right stuff. Sure, if you had asked me at the time I would have replied emphatically that there was nothing more critical than building a suite of materials and having a drawer full of product and programs ready for Clients at a moment's notice. I missed the point entirely, and it is not beyond the realm of possibilities that I was performing the work I was comfortable with. Not unlike a newly promoted people manager, who when faced with a new human resource challenge, and lacking the necessary experience to draw upon, will often revert back to performing the technical work they used to do, at least feeling comfortable and accomplished in their functional capability even though this is not the work that is required of them anymore.

The crux for leaders everywhere is that we must find, refine or develop our ability to adapt to the times in which we find ourselves. In my early career I had similar frustrations as I approached my new boss, concerned that I was not in fact skilled for the job I had taken on. My manager at the time advised me wisely that my skills were not in question. The task ahead of me now was to apply those skills in this new environment "yes you can do this work, and now you have to do it here."

We talk extensively at Lake about the importance of developing and implementing a Plan (see Chapter One) and of the six reasons we suggest to Clients as to why they should have a Plan in the first place is to make sure everyone is busy doing the right work, and not just busy being busy. Your willing team will want to work hard for you in most cases, however they may not always want to do the work that you want them to do.

Concentrating upon and rewarding effort for output, and valuing a quality end result, are not new concepts in the world of management. This philosophy however can, on occasion, be overshadowed by an insistence to control the situation and impose meaningless measures on productivity and industriousness, and time is usually the perfect and most visible example. We can literally see someone putting the time in.

My first job, after leaving Manchester Polytechnic in 1990, took me to central London. The pervasive culture of the organization where I worked was an hours culture that valued arriving in the office at 7:30am and not leaving much before 8pm. This was, as I mentioned, my first grown-up job and as such I was not comfortable to challenge the established norms, despite having a one hour commute at either end of the day as I lived in Kingston at the time. Add to this the fact that the job did not in any way demand 12 hours worth of daily input five days a week. My solution to this ridiculousness was to wander up and down Oxford Street in the middle of the afternoon, going for coffee, and literally trying to pass the time so I could save up work to do in the evening and be seated at my desk looking busy as if I too absolutely had to stay late to keep up, just like everybody else. I wonder if any of the others were doing likewise?

*From the Lake Blog May 3, 2010: The Employee, The
Customer, and Ah Yes, You, The Leader*

*In service based industries, and for the most part we in the west
are deeply rooted in service driven economies, the delivery of the
service to the customer occurs in real-time, sometimes referred to
as the Moment of Truth. The effective execution of the service
encounter is a key challenge for all service driven organizations as
they attempt to control the large number of variables at play during
this interaction. In 1978, Sasser, Olsen and Wyckoff identified
the unique characteristics of services, namely simultaneity,
heterogeneity, intangibility and perishability; highlighting that by
their very nature, service operations present complex managerial
challenges. Simultaneity is perhaps the most pressing of these
challenges from a leadership perspective as the production and
consumption of the service occur in real-time (ibid). Get it wrong,
and you get it wrong in front of the customer. Thirty years later
and inevitably leaders are still attempting to influence the service
encounter compounded by the fact that today's leaders are usually
trying to do so from a physical distance. Whether geographically
driven or not, leaders in service sectors remain firmly on the
outside of the customer / employee interaction. The expertise
of leaders within service organizations can be greatly tested as
the behaviour of employees and the reactions of the consumer
continue to be the unspoken influences on overall service success.
The practical leadership implications presented by such realities
are numerous, daunting and difficult to meet without focused
effort. Employees can be trained in customer service, selling, and
even in problem resolution, yet the real-time delivery challenge
remains. We argue that while training provides the how for
a given task, effective coaching creates an environment that*

demands superior performance. If you are relying on exceptional results from an interaction that you as a leader cannot see, but your customers can, then you have to coach for it.

Creating the space, carving out the time and giving yourself and your team room to breath can be precisely the time when the best work happens. How many of us keep a pad and pen by the bed for that middle of the night idea inspiration? How many of us leave ourselves a voice mail while watching kids play hockey as brilliance strikes our imaginations at the start of the second period?

Lovely Husband and I recently took ourselves out for a lazy lunch one Friday afternoon to a local pub after several days in a row locked in the home office, diligently working hard and eating almost every meal at the desk. The joy of leaving the office, added to the change of atmosphere, and became a catalyst for our creativity, and, because we talk about work much of the time, over chicken wings and coffee we developed an entirely new marketing plan for Lake, which incidentally was implemented almost immediately and is working very nicely. I cannot tell you how many good ideas come to me on the drive home from yoga, or when drying my hair, chopping onions, or walking Molly. I am more productive and more effective when I am busy, active and engaged, and when my interests are varied. This does not mean one can forego the discipline of work. In writing this book I set daily word counts and kept to them even if the next day I had to go back and rewrite the whole thing, it didn't matter, I had to see words on a page. I didn't measure the time I put in I measured the pages completed and then later the quality of those pages. Had I not implemented this disciplined approach to writing I would still be bleating on about how I was planning to write a book, and to paraphrase the Tragically Hip, no one cares about the stuff you had every good intention of doing, but didn't.

From the Food Diary

August 22—weight 137lbs—75 minutes yoga

- All Bran, muesli, milk, blueberries
- Beef curry and rice
- 2 glasses of wine
- 9 squares of Dairy Milk

August 23—weight 137lbs—60 minutes yoga

- All Bran, muesli, milk
- Chilli, 2 Ryvita with butter and Branston pickle
- 3 glasses of wine
- Many squares of Dairy Milk

August 24

- Blueberry muffin
- Tin tuna, mayo, 3 x Ryvita
- Tin of chickpeas, with salt & Tabasco, straight out of the can
- 2 glasses of wine

August 25—weight 136lbs—75 minutes yoga

- All Bran, muesli, blackberries, milk
- Chilli
- 2 glasses of wine

CHAPTER 9
BE AMAZING

"Literature is strewn with the wreckage of men
Who have minded beyond reason the opinions of others."

Virginia Wolf

When Hannah left us to return to the UK as planned on Monday September 7, her next big adventure was to leave home and start University the following month as a first year undergraduate. The only fleetingly positive element of the entirely ghastly heart-wrenching airport goodbye (as the movies say we are all so much better at hellos) was that a member of the ground crew threw me a sympathetic I-know-what-you're-going-through look as Lovely Husband and I flanking Hannah strode through Terminal 3 looking like parents seeing our daughter off to college. Admittedly that felt good for a moment. Following several false departures, false starts at attempting to leave her but in reverse you understand, Lovely Husband and I arrived back at our home and talked about what a fine young woman Hannah is and how although we had loved having her with us for every single minute, it was now Hannah's job to go out into the world and be amazing.

What do Prince Harry, Agatha Christie, Tommy Lee Jones, Oliver Stone, Marco Polo, Sophie Dahl, and I have in common? A shared birthday, of September 15 actually, which makes me (and them) a Virgo, if you believe in that sort of thing, and actually still a Virgo even if you don't and on occasion I confess I do, believe that is. When I am supposed to be working, and evidently failing, I will diligently look up my daily horoscope on various newspaper websites, usually until I find an outlook I can live with. To save you the trouble, The Toronto Star is, in my experience, much more positive and optimistic in the horoscope arena than all the other papers, which, again in my opinion, deliver only gloomy predictions and dire warnings. After reading some of these grim offerings (putting the horror in horoscope) I feel I should either go back to bed and stay there until the moon in Pisces moves out of my galactic influence, or at the very least say "nothing to no one" for the remainder of the day.

Having trawled the zodiac sites, and no doubt having been advised by a professional horoscope forecaster to stop scouring the internet and get on with some bloody work, if I am still unable to crack on with the task at hand I will look up Lovely Husband's (Pisces), My Sister's (Aries), various friends and family members (Capricorns, Scorpios, Cancers, Sagittarians, Leos, Taureans) and even Molly's (Gemini in case you were wondering). Based on this extensive research, Virgos, again in my opinion, always get something of a bad rap in the horoscope world as we are painted as the worriers, the neat freaks, the critics, and the cool exterior perfectionists. How do you like me so far? Furthermore on the days when I read just about everyone's horoscope, Virgos frequently seem to be in for a rough day when compared to the carefree easy come easy going signs, which incidentally covers just about all non-Virgoans. I do believe if I am not mistaken, that we Virgos are in possession of some strong points, however you have to comb the zodiac literature quite extensively to find them.

Inviting workshop participants to list their abilities and ignore their limitations is invariably a fascinating exercise. Not sure if it is a Canadian thing, so I will resist the cultural stereotypes, however, in my experience adult learners often struggle when asked to talk about the things at which they excel. When, after some coaxing and encouragement, the workshop attendees do manage to come up with a list of strengths it is not unusual to see that these so called strengths are in fact re-packaged weaknesses. For example, a manager, who was part of a team I was facilitating one morning at the front end of a day of goal setting, commented that he was really good at no longer messing up spreadsheets. Women in particular, again based on my experience, cite domestic successes, e.g. I'm a good cook. Odd choices for a work setting, and few participants, if any, claimed to be a strong leader, a good manager, an excellent communicator or marketing genius, and yet in practice many of them were extremely talented and damned good at their jobs.

I don't know if this is just the light under a bushel stuff we talked about earlier in Chapter 7, not sure, so what I think is relevant here is that these people are highly capable and as such just get on with it. Why? Because? It was of little or no consequence who was asking, or who was observing. Feeling a sense of confidence in one's own abilities and acting on that confidence is a powerful force. Not caring what others think of you, of your skills, talents, traits, decisions and life choices, is to be liberated from the Approval Grip.

Virgos are apparently society's critics, and yet to be immune to the criticism of outsiders is a state worth pursuing and probably especially important for a Virgo. If we Virgoans feel less criticized maybe we shall in turn criticize less. You cannot prevent others from holding positive and or negative opinions about you but you can choose to let those opinions go. As Lovely Husband says, opinions / ears / everyone / got them.

The Approval Grip, just to explore this concept for a moment, is a veritable Bermuda Triangle for success, happiness, fulfillment and peace. I have not spent any time in my adult years reading passages from the Bible, even when deadly bored in the too-hot-to-sleep-air-conditioning-too-loud middle of the night in the middle of nowhere sweltering California hotels during the Budget years. I was however, a regular at the Poulton-le-Fylde Methodist Church Sunday School from the age of nothing to about 14, so I do have some scripturous teachings etched on my brain. One story I do remember learning at Sunday school, although even I know it is in fact a Fable, is the tale of the Miller, his Son and their Donkey. As the trio passed through a number of towns, onlookers would offer comments and sly quips along the lines of why was the boy riding the donkey and the father walking, and then vice versa. This continued as you may remember, until the bloody idiot Miller and his not much better Son, thoroughly fed up with all the chastisements from the good townsfolk they encountered, ended up carrying the ass between them and feeling like, well, you know, total arses. Aesop is teaching us all no doubt to ignore the critics and go your own way, carve your own path, and carry your own damned donkey if you want to. This is all well and good, and as advice goes I would rank it an eight out of ten.

My general advice is to yes, yes, floss, eat your greens, get 8 hours beauty rest every night, exercise your body, vote, work hard, laugh, love and call your Mother, but my top ten highest advice ranking is to Be Amazing. I firmly believe this is the highest compliment we can receive and how could you fail to appreciate yourself, and others, when you consider them to, and they return the compliment of considering you to, Be Amazing. I used to think that to be described as fearless was the top drawer, and I agree it is still up there, but I'll take amazing over fearless. Try it out for size, go on, sing along with me, my name is *(insert your name here)* and I am AMAZING. Feels pretty good, no? Now, the trick is to go out there and live up to this, yeah, so good luck with that one! I'm kidding, come on, we can do this together.

Asim Biswas (pronounced Osh-eem), of Kolkata, West Bengal, born eldest child to Kritanta and Lela Biswas in 1928, a former Brigadier in the Indian Army, husband, brother, father, grandfather, and uncle, died at his daughter Jasmine's house on September 14, 2010 in Washington DC while on holiday with his wife. I had not seen my Uncle Asim, or Jethu as My Sister and I called him, meaning father's elder brother, since I was last in India in 1996. We were not close. Regardless of the lack of depth in this particular familial relationship I was the only relative on the same continent at the time of his death (after his wife and daughter, Jasmine my cousin, of course). It is not easy for Indians to obtain visas to visit the US at short notice and it was highly unlikely that Jasmine's brothers or anyone else from the extended family, my own Father of course living in the UK, could be with Jasmine and her immediate family at this time, and in time for a Hindu funeral.

Lovely Husband and I received the news of Asim's sudden death, looked at our calendars, got on the phones, were grateful to be able to rearrange various meetings, grateful for once that Molly was at her city residence, and on September 15 we drove to Washington to be with Jasmine, and her Mum. This is not however, emphatically not, the story of claiming how amazing we were to jump in the car and hit the highway. We were fortunate to be able to do this and not in any way exceptional, you would have done the same thing. The amazing person here is Jasmine, who for as long as I shall live will forever in my eyes, Be Amazing.

Lovely Husband and I crossed into the US at Fort Erie, Ontario, and drove south for around nine hours which included a couple of stops along the way for some really terrible food. I am sure there are perfectly splendid places to eat in Pennsylvania and Virginia but it is safe to say we missed all of them. We did encounter a couple of buses carrying a group of Amish folks whom we observed doing a number at a service stop Burger King. This was a sight to lift your soul as the young people among the crowd, the boys in their blue shirts and black pants, the girls in their long cotton dresses and modest hats, chattered animatedly discussing with anticipation their BK menu choices.

The weather throughout the day of September 15 was warm and clear offering spectacular views of Pennsylvania in particular. We arrived without incident at Jasmine's place around 6pm. Given that I had not seen Asim since 1996 this was also the last time I had seen Jasmine, despite the fact that she had moved to the US from India around 2004 with her fabulous husband Dakshi (whom Lovely Husband and I adored on sight). When I was last in India in October 1996, I had been on a working trip as part of a British Universities whirlwind tour of the country, with an insane itinerary of something like 6 Indian cities in 9 days, in an attempt to persuade bright young Indian students to come and study for their Postgraduate degrees and MBAs in the UK. Prior to collecting me from my hotel to join the family for dinner, in then Calcutta, Jethu and Jasmine had seen me on the telly appearing on the local news, I felt very famous and glamorous. Shame on all of us, for not keeping in touch but there was no time for that now.

So here is Jasmine, with her Mother a new widow of 24 hours, her full of beans totally adorable six year old daughter Mina, the wonderfully dependable Dakshi, and a Hindu funeral to arrange for the next day for her Indian father who was one minute on holiday visiting his youngest child, granddaughter and son-in-law and the next being cremated in a country not of his birth or residence.

To say Jasmine is capable, calm and focused is like saying Bill Clinton is a decent after dinner speaker. She was nothing shy of amazing. I should add that Jasmine and Dakshi each hold down pretty demanding jobs and like most young couples starting out with a young family are more or less run ragged every minute of the day every day of the week. Oh yes and now the long lost cousin and Lovely Husband have arrived from Canada. Actually she was thrilled to see us but you can only imagine.

The morning of the funeral was sunny and gorgeous. Jasmine and Dakshi had managed to locate and hire the services of a Hindu priest, who had actually met Asim on a previous visit to USA. At 11am Jasmine, her Mother, husband Dakshi, daughter Mina, Lovely Husband and I, we celebrated Asim's life together in a tony suburb of DC. Following the service and cremation, little of which Lovely Husband and I understood, although Dakshi tried his best to explain, I hugged Jasmine, and told her how amazing I thought she was. Jasmine hugged me back, her face a portrait of composure and resolve, and without any betrayal of emotion whatsoever replied evenly "Well Rash it is what it is." Now that is amazing. That was an amazing woman under dreadful circumstances smoothly carrying out the duties required with love, efficiency, grace, and without fear.

Later that afternoon, Lovely Husband and I drove home in a frightful and relentless full-on windscreen wipers all the way rainstorm, still managing to miss all the good eats, and spending much of our journey in silence.

To Be Amazing, in my view, requires one to be Authentic, Resourceful, Inspiring, Noble, Kind, and Young-at-Heart. The basis for supporting, and for selecting this particular half dozen of wordy ingredients, is solely grounded in my own experience, and with a nod to my cousin Jasmine to whom I owe the inspiration and the mnemonic itself.

Authentic: Knowing who you are, being true to yourself, acknowledging the talents you have, and bravely developing the ones that will benefit you and others, is what it means to me to be authentic. Being who you are, or indeed who you are supposed to be, is without doubt, the first step towards becoming amazing. After all you want to be amazing as you. As the sex store in Toronto of the same name proudly boast and strongly urge us all to "Come As You Are." Think of someone you know whom you consider to Be Amazing and twenty dollars says they are authentically and unapologetically themselves. I appreciate the talents of others both known and unknown to me, however I am at my best when being just Rash. I sometimes hear my fake laugh, or phony stretched screeches of pretend and feigned interest, and I shudder inwardly. I am without doubt a much more interesting, engaging, not necessarily likeable, and overall calmer soul when I permit me to be me. I say not necessarily likeable although in truth I don't know if this is the case. I am aware that on occasion I will put on this front in order to appear likable so I assume when I drop the act I am no longer likable. The part however that I am unclear on is whether any of that façade stuff works or everyone can see through me anyway, not sure. What I am sure about however, is that I am at my best when I am authentic.

Beyond practicing the art of authenticity as a desire to be ourselves, we must additionally endeavour to become (and remain) trustworthy, reliable and true to others, all equally worthy definitions of authentic. The dual responsibility here lies in being true to ourselves (genuine) and being true to others (honest). Authenticity is not an insignificant challenge to set oneself on the quest to Be Amazing, however it's a pretty fine place to start. I can say that in deciding to be authentically me my relationship with My Sister has improved beyond all recognition, as has my career, my health, and my overall sense of self and purpose.

Resourceful: Coping with life's little, and not so little surprises demands a high degree of resourcefulness. Being able to cope with whatever happens and knowing that you are confident in your ability to deal is key. If you are resourceful you worry less, you do more (with less), you eliminate your fears, and you see opportunities where others see problems. This is the *Stockdale Paradox* (Collins, 2001) in action. I am in awe of the late Vice Admiral James Bond Stockdale, and suspect you are familiar with his story, and equally in awe. Briefly, Jim Stockdale was the highest-ranking US Naval Officer to be held as a Prisoner of War during the Vietnam War and as such was imprisoned for eight years. For the full account read the original work in *Good to Great* by Jim Collins. However the summary of what Collins termed the *Stockdale Paradox* based on Jim Stockdale's harrowing experience as a POW is to face the harsh reality of your situation and at the same time know that you will overcome. The lesson is to accept that we cannot blindly assume we will be okay whatever happens to us yet nor can we become swallowed by our anguish and fears. We have to do both, hence the paradox.

Learning to become more resourceful is a developable skill available to all. As my top man bother-in-law often comments "keep saying yes until they give you a reason to say no." Clive generally uses this in terms of employment opportunities and work related projects however I am borrowing it here in support of being resourceful. Saying yes instead of saying no. In Organizational Development speak we continually advise Clients that if you want to change the culture (of a company) then, among other things, you need to change the language. Think back to the OWN network example of excluding certain words. In business if you wish to refocus a service team towards sales, then change their job titles, rename the reports they receive and recast the meetings with an agenda laden with language reflective of the new direction. This approach of changing the language to change the culture can be readily applied to a variety of situations both professional and personal. With that in mind, if you wish to train yourself to become more resourceful, start with action oriented sentences. When faced with a problem try saying out loud (sotto voce if you prefer) "I am going to come up with three ideas as to how I can handle this" which will focus the thinking for your new and tough situation rather than have you glaring wild-eyed into the mirror like a mad woman wondering how in the name of all things sane you are going to get through. This will challenge you to search out what you can do instead of assuming that you can't. This is truly "getting out of your own way." As Lovely Husband frequently challenges "tell me what you do want, not what you don't want." I confess it is usually easier to come up with the negative list as we can often be lazy after all. Saying what it is you do want to happen instead of listing what it is you don't want to happen takes work no question, but the pay off is far greater. By identifying the outcome you desire you then have a fighting chance of achieving that outcome.

Inspiring: Okay, I agree this sounds like a tall order however it need not be a monumental inspiration such as is the stuff of Guinness World Records or acts of heroism that most of us are unlikely to encounter during an average trip to the movies, day at the office or quick dash to the grocery store. We can inspire each other on a daily basis with plenty of seemingly small gestures. After a conversation with my friend Luke I might be inspired to cook a new dish as whenever we speak on the phone (almost daily) Luke usually fills me in on what is on the menu that night in the Woods-Marshall household. Reading an email from My Sister usually inspires me to make weekend plans. A meeting over coffee with a colleague or business acquaintance can often inspire me to read a new business book or article. Sometimes even seeing a well-dressed woman inspires me to raise my game and put on some lipstick. And as dog owners the world over know all too well, seeing the way your puppy adores you cannot help but inspire us to be even a fraction of the superhuman that she believes us to be.

Noble: In this context noble equates grace. Facing the inevitable knowing you have explored all remaining courses of action and accepting the decisions you have made or perhaps have been made for you requires grace. Accepting and moving on without assigning blame to others or harbouring resentment is noble indeed. I left a tough job once, correction it was a great job, however it had become a difficult job within an increasingly tough environment and it was time to move on. I remember vividly my leaving and that on my last day several colleagues posted a flipchart on my office door and scrawled upon it delightful and kind comments of the things they had learned from me during our time together. One person dryly commented that she learned from me that you *could* in fact wear pearls with everything. Another wrote that I had taught her how to be graceful under pressure. I recognized and valued the compliment for what it was, and I took it with me when I moved on.

Kind: It rather goes without saying that if you are to be amazing you must be a decent human being. We are striving for amazing in a good way here, not amazing as in bizarre. Being kind to others is surprisingly easy and yet we find ourselves executing this small daily and readily accessible act with startling infrequency. I am fond of the expression "random acts of kindness" and do believe it to be contagious. Try a random act of kindness today and see what happens.

When Lovely Husband and I visited Sasha in Paris a couple of years ago we were taking the subway back to Sasha's place fairly late one Friday night. At the turnstile ahead of us a middle aged American couple were frantically searching for money and becoming more and more anxious as they realized the late hour, the growing crowd behind them and their less than bright predicament as they searched fruitlessly for an elusive wallet. It felt good to see the relief on their faces as we paid their fares and sent them safely on their way, and as they ran ahead to catch their train they called back to us insisting that they too would do something nice for someone else and send a collective thank you out into the universe.

My wonderful friend Diane usually arrives with delicious food whenever she visits our house. Sometimes the homemade granola or the exotic fruit salad is in a lovely one of a kind dish or plate, and Diane always insists we are to enjoy the food and pass the plate along. There is never a requirement or expectation to return the crockery. I love the idea of all these pieces of tableware doing the rounds over the years and finding different homes in different kitchens at various times in their lives, and all the more appealing is that they were given freely and not because we were neglectful in their return.

Young-at-Heart: I hold great admiration for all those who are unabashedly Young-at-Heart, particularly as I am not quite there yet. Playful, eager, curious, creative, energetic, non-ego driven, confident and adventurous, the sure fire indicators of someone who is definitively Young-at-Heart. I believe this is our ideal paradigm in the quest to Be Amazing. To be Young-at-Heart brings with it an aura of invincibility and a slight smirk to the lips making everyone else wonder what you've been up to and secretly wishing whatever it is they wish they had been up to it too.

To Be Amazing is something of an elusive quality and clearly open to the interpretation of the beholder. Young-at-Heart grants us the similar option. What is childlike to one is childish to another. What is one person's confidence is another's arrogance. Having said that, being Young-at-Heart is a state of mind where we open our hearts, our souls and equally importantly we open our minds. When I first became a manager I was calling a member of my team who was off sick and recovering at home. Following the HR rules at the appointed day and time I was to call this person to keep her up to date on general issues and to inquire about her progress. When I called the house, a young child answered the phone; I asked to speak to Mummy and told the young receptionist that I was Rashmi. I heard the phone clang back down on to the table and small footsteps speed away calling to her Mother that "Muuh-mm-eee, Rash-meee is on the phone." I cannot tell you how many times I have said my name to an adult stranger only for them to pull a face, mangle my name and look at me as if I were spewing up a dead crocodile into their lap. A two year old with a fresh perspective and no learned prejudice simply repeats what she has heard, without judgment. Oh yes I want to be Young-at-Heart.

If you do not consider yourself to Be Amazing then here are some key questions to ask:

1. If you are not amazing, then what would it take for you to Be Amazing?
2. If you know what it would take then why don't you do it?
3. If you don't know what it would take, ask someone who loves you, they probably think you already are amazing.

From the Food Diary

September 7—DNW (Dare Not Weigh)—60 minutes yoga

- All Bran, muesli, milk, blueberries
- Plums, tomatoes, almonds
- Dahl, ½ tin chick peas
- 1 gin & tonic
- 1 glass of wine

September 8—136lbs—75 minutes yoga

- All Bran, muesli, milk, blueberries
- ½ tin chickpeas
- 1 apple
- 1 burger, handful of almonds
- 2 glasses of wine

September 9—136 lbs—60 minutes yoga

- All Bran, muesli, milk, blueberries
- Apple, almonds
- 3 slices pizza
- 2 glasses of wine

*From the Lake Blog September 14, 2011: Passion, Principles
and Pink Cadillacs*

*Named "Most Outstanding Woman in Business in the 20th
Century" by Lifetime Television in 1999 Mary Kay was an
astonishing success. Last night the Business Book Club met to
review "The Mary Kay Way" coincidentally on the very day
when Mary Kay launched her incredible cosmetics business
48 years ago in Dallas. Having now read and I might add
thoroughly enjoyed the book I am astonished by Mary Kay's
courage, determination, unwavering principles and ability
to translate her own values into a brilliant business model
against unbelievable odds. Let's just think for a moment about
a woman starting her own cosmetics business in 1963, then
let's reflect on how Mary Kay defeated her critics, drew upon
her self-belief, worked hard and created defining disciplines.
Perhaps the strongest message in the book is Mary Kay's
unwavering philosophy of valuing people and being able to
translate this value into a management philosophy of treating
everyone with respect in a climate of sharing and support, all
at a time when I suspect these were not the standard operating
rules of the day. Imagine the conferences, that are to this day,
according to a friend of mine a long time Mary Kay Beauty
Consultant, the most professional and inspiring events where
women at their own expense in terms of time and travel costs
voluntarily participate to learn, and grow, maximizing the
opportunity to motivate themselves and others. Imagine having
that sense of commitment not because you are an employee and
it is in your job description to show up and wave the corporate
flag but because you are passionate about your business, your
company and your leader. Surely for a leader there is no higher*

measure of success. One of the delights in my job is interviewing fascinating entrepreneurial women for the L.I.F.E. series. I wish I could have interviewed Mary Kay and heard her responses to our nine questions. However, in the absence of that, read her book, I know we all still have much to learn from the "Most Outstanding Woman in Business in the 20th Century."

EPILOGUE

Originally when I set out to chart and record the life changing transitions of 2010 and in particular the move from corporate employment to self-employment I had considered using the tried, tested and perhaps tired method and format of a monthly diary, and I fully expected the book would comprise the requisite twelve chapters. As a fastidious INTJ, in Myers-Briggs speak, I had each chapter mapped out and I was focused upon capturing the linear process of my experience and noting the monthly changes as if I were a broad bean pressed up against a piece of pink blotting paper inside a jam jar being monitored by a junior school class for the science project. I had genuinely believed I could chart my growth and measure my sprouting wings with scientific precision and that all of this would of course take place in accordance with the calendar. This would have been highly convenient and extremely tidy, and very OCD of me.

Unsurprisingly the changes we encounter, the decisions we make and the direction we take is not always a logical exercise or process. Absolutely we can apply logic to decision making during the in-the-moment thought process. For example, Lovely Husband is currently working with a hypnotherapist to help him give up smoking. The therapist advised Lovely Husband that the decision to have a cigarette takes six seconds. Perhaps all decisions take only six seconds, the researchers can no doubt tell us more. I suspect the pondering stage of the decision making process where we are weighing up the pros and cons of a particular course of action takes the bulk of our time and it is here that we waver and wobble.

To overcome such wavering and wobbling, we need a Plan, followed by making the single Decision to execute the Plan.

Having gone through the experience of making a significant life change in 2010 (and in other years) and then writing about it, I am more convinced than ever that an essential tool needed by all to navigate life is a Plan. Certainly it is what I needed. If we take the time to assess our values, conduct our own personal SWOT analysis, and identify the vision for our life, then we can make decisions to serve us well. There is no question that real life will get in the way of perfectly executing our Plan on a daily basis, but it is the Plan that will bring us back on track, and provide us with the confidence to believe in ourselves when the negative Nelly is gnawing away at our self-esteem. The singular best decision we can make is to decide to develop a thoughtful Plan. Next January when you conduct your own *Year in Review*, which most of us do to a greater or lesser extent, we can Plan to reflect on a year that held fewer disappointments and more positive outcomes.

Lovely Husband and I recently watched the touchingly sad movie *Another Year* directed by the talented Mike Leigh. The lesson for me in watching this film was how little life can change unless we become active participants in charting our own course. Unless we take responsibility, and more importantly take action, our life will just happen to us, and frankly that is a frightening prospect.

I remember leaving Manchester Polytechnic in July 1990 and being asked by one of the academic staff during our final session what our future held for us as individuals. I had no idea what my future held for me nor did I know what I wanted it to look like and so I was scrambling for a made up response. From the back rows one supremely confident student stated loudly that he fully intended to be Captain of his own ship. He probably is. So am I. And you can be too.

REFERENCES: BOOKS

Ash, Mary Kay. 2008. *The Mary Kay Way: Timeless Principles from America's Greatest Woman Entrepreneur.* New Jersey: Wiley

Collins, Jim. 2001. *Good to Great.* New York: Harper Collins.

Jeffers, Susan. 1988. *Feel the Fear and Do It Anyway.* Toronto: Random House.

Johnson, Spencer. 1998. *Who Moved My Cheese?* New York: Putnam.

Mallick, Heather. 2004. *Pearls in Vinegar.* Toronto: Viking.

Myers, Isabel Briggs with Peter B. Myers. 1980. *Gifts Differing.* Palo Alto: Consulting Psychologists Press

Sanders, Tim. 2002. *Love is the Killer App.* New York: Random House.

Sasser, W. Earl, Olsen, R. Paul & D. Daryl Wyckoff. 1978. *Management of Service Operations.* Boston: Allyn and Bacon.

Westen, Drew. 2007.*The Political Brain.* New York: PublicAffairs.

REFERENCES: ARTICLES

Coyne, Andrew. January 11, 2011. *Stuck in Traffic*. Maclean's Magazine.

Draper, Doug. January 25, 2010. *Niagara Network Calls on Ontario Government to Focus More Attention on People's Basic Needs*. Niagara At Large: http://niagaraatlarge.com/

Economist. January 21, 2010. *Absolutely: Power Corrupts, But It Corrupts Only Those Who Think They Deserve It*.

REFERENCES: MOVIES

Another Year. Directed by Mike Leigh. UK, 2010.

Bend It Like Beckham. Directed by Gurinder Chadha. UK, 2002.

In Bruges. Directed by Martin McDonagh. UK, 2008.

Nowhere Boy. Directed by Sam Taylor-Wood. UK, 2009.

Sleeping With The Enemy. Directed by Joseph Ruben. USA, 1991.

When Harry Met Sally. Directed by Rob Reiner. USA, 1989.

REFERENCES: SONGS

Blue Rodeo. *Never Look Back*. Album: The Things We Left Behind. Warner, 2009.

Bowie, David. *Changes*. Album: Hunky Dory. RCA Records, 1972.

Gray, David. *Sail Away*. Album: White Ladder. IHT Records, 2001.

Gray, David. *The Other Side*. Album: A New Day At Midnight. EastWest, 2002.

Queen. *Radio Ga Ga*. Album: The Works. EMI/Capitol, 1984.

Reid, Johnny. *Today I'm Gonna Try And Change The World*. Album: A Place Called Love. EMI, 2010.

Rufus and Chaka Khan. *Tell Me Something Good*. Album: Rags to Rufus. ABC Records, 1974.

The Rolling Stones. *You Can't Always Get What You Want*. Album: Let it Bleed. Decca Records, 1969.

The Smiths. *Meat is Murder*. Album: Meat is Murder. Rough Trade, 1985.

The Tragically Hip. *Wheat Kings*. Album: Fully Completely. MCA, 1992.

Waits, Tom: *Martha*. Album: Closing Time. Asylum, 1973.

ACKNOWLEDGEMENTS

I have many people to thank for their love, support and enthusiasm, including, Shyamali Fenton, Douglas Hotte, Daniel Le Blanc, Clive Fenton, Nandini Biswas Das, Ana Davies, Ursula James, Ilse Besteman, Donna Londry, Monika Evans, Hannah Robinson and Alex Robinson. Some of you read earlier versions of the book, some of you were on-demand editors and proof readers, and all of you gave me the encouragement I needed to keep writing and self-publish. I must thank my parents Ann and Prasanta Biswas for, among other things, giving me my early love of books, and for not pressing me to read draft versions of *Rash Decisions*. Somehow you knew I wanted you to see it for the first time as a finished product. The members of NABWN for welcoming me into the fold and helping to cure my fear of networking. The members of the Niagara Business Book Club for enthusing greatly when I revealed I had written a book. Tracey Turavani from Sensible Office Services for her calm and professional administrative expertise, and Balboa Press for their help and guidance. And above all I owe so much to Rick Besteman, my Lovely Husband. Rick read each chapter as it came off the printer, proclaiming it to be "superlative" and declaring that he couldn't wait for the next one. How could I not succeed with the best coach in the country at my side? Thank you seems pretty small after all you have done and continue to do for me Rick. I remain your Number One Fan.